T0051536

'This step-by-step approach can be tackled in brief chunks of time. It is easy to read and includes lots of inspiring and fun exercises to help you on your journey to developing healthy habits. Although written for young people, it's a must-read for any age.'

– Professor Trudie Chalder, Kings College London, former chair of the British Association for Behavioural & Cognitive Psychotherapies

'The perfect book for your school's mental health library for young people. One of the best self-help books for young people I have come across.'

– Veronika Chidemo, former assistant head, designated senior mental health lead and Youth Mental Health First Aid instructor and consultant

of related interest

No Weigh!
A Teen's Guide to Positive Body Image, Food, and Emotional Wisdom
Signe Darpinian, Wendy Sterling and Shelley Aggarwal
Foreword by Connie Sobczak
ISBN 978 1 78592 825 3
eISBN 978 1 78450 946 0

The Mental Health and Wellbeing Workout for Teens
Skills and Exercises from ACT and CBT for Healthy Thinking
Paula Nagel
Illustrated by Gary Bainbridge
ISBN 978 1 78592 394 4
eISBN 978 1 78450 753 4

My Intense Emotions Handbook
Manage Your Emotions and Connect Better with Others
Sue Knowles, Bridie Gallagher and Hannah Bromley
Illustrated by Emmeline Pidgen
Foreword by Kim Golding
ISBN 978 1 78775 382 2
eISBN 978 1 78775 383 9

My Anxiety Handbook
Sue Knowles, Bridie Gallagher and Phoebe McEwen
Illustrated by Emmeline Pidgen
ISBN 978 1 78592 440 8
eISBN 978 1 78450 813 5

The Healthy Coping Colouring Book and Journal
Creative Activities to Help Manage Stress, Anxiety and Other Big Feelings
Pooky Knightsmith
Illustrated by Emily Hamilton
ISBN 978 1 78592 139 1
eISBN 978 1 78450 405 2

You Can Change the World!
Everyday Teen Heroes Making a Difference Everywhere
Margaret Rooke
Forewords by Taylor Richardson and Katie Hodgetts @KTclimate
Illustrated by Kara McHale
ISBN 978 1 78592 502 3
eISBN 978 1 78450 897 5

10 MINUTES TO BETTER MENTAL HEALTH

A Step-by-Step Guide for Teens Using CBT and Mindfulness

Lee David and Debbie Brewin

Illustrated by Rebecca Price

Jessica Kingsley Publishers
London and Philadelphia

First published in Great Britain in 2022 by Jessica Kingsley Publishers
An imprint of Hodder & Stoughton Ltd
An Hachette Company

1

Copyright © Lee David and Debbie Brewin 2022

The right of Lee David and Debbie Brewin to be identified as the Authors of the Work has
been asserted by them in accordance with the Copyright, Designs and Patents Act 1988.

All rights reserved. No part of this publication may be reproduced, stored in a retrieval system,
or transmitted, in any form or by any means without the prior written permission of the
publisher, nor be otherwise circulated in any form of binding or cover other than that in which
it is published and without a similar condition being imposed on the subsequent purchaser.

Additional material can be downloaded for personal use with this program, but may
not be reproduced for any other purposes without the permission of the publisher.

Disclaimer: *The information contained in this book is not intended to replace the services of
trained medical professionals or to be a substitute for medical advice. The complementary therapy
described in this book may not be suitable for everyone to follow. You are advised to consult a
doctor before embarking on any complementary therapy programme and on any matters relating
to your health, and in particular on any matters that may require diagnosis or medical attention.*

A CIP catalogue record for this title is available from the British Library and the Library of Congress

ISBN 978 1 78775 556 7
eISBN 978 1 78775 570 3

Printed and bound in Great Britain by TJ Books Limited

Jessica Kingsley Publishers' policy is to use papers that are natural, renewable and recyclable
products and made from wood grown in sustainable forests. The logging and manufacturing
processes are expected to conform to the environmental regulations of the country of origin.

Jessica Kingsley Publishers
Carmelite House
50 Victoria Embankment
London EC4Y 0DZ

www.jkp.com

Contents

Acknowledgements

Appreciation goes to my extended family for inspiration and support and to the many young people I have had the privilege of working alongside on their journey to positive mental health. Gratitude goes to Lee for the opportunity to write with her and to the publishers for their belief in this book.

Debbie Brewin

A huge thanks and appreciation to my family for their encouragement, support and love, which always keeps going through the challenges of balancing all the different priorities in life. Thank you to Debbie for being a wonderful partner in writing and developing the ideas that contributed to this book and many other projects over many years. And to all the young people I have worked with who are the inspiration for this book, and the publisher and editors for their patience and support in taking this book from concept to reality.

Lee David

INTRODUCTION

→ Have you found your direction and purpose in life, or are you floundering – anxious and aimless like you've lost your phone?

→ Are you comfortable in your group, or do you compare yourself unfavourably and maybe even avoid friends?

→ Have you fallen into the trap of reacting angrily towards others when you feel criticised, or does low mood get in the way of you doing things?

→ Have you got 10 minutes? Read on...

 **Read This** 🕐 **10 Minutes**

What is this book about?

This book will help you to get the best out of life. It is a practical workbook made up of information, advice, videos and exercises. We use a framework called 10 Minute GROW, which helps keep things brief, to the point and easy to remember.

With this book, you can choose to spend 10 minutes a day moving yourself and your life in the direction that **you** want to take.

We aim to provide skills to help you navigate your way through difficulties and become the person you want to be. With the pressures of school, college and exams, no one has time to spend ages doing anything extra, so we've broken it down into bite-sized chunks and use a variety of media to help.

Find it hard to believe that just 10 minutes a day can help? Well, we believe that there are many reasons that you might find this book helpful: we have based the information and exercises on research evidence from reliable sources, and we include concrete examples of how you might use or apply these ideas.

Understand the science

→ The average attention span is 10–20 minutes, so we provide information in bite-size chunks, with timings, so you know how long each section will take.

→ We all learn new skills by trying things out, noticing what happened, adjusting and repeating – so we will ask you to take action, find out what works best for you and work out how you can bring this into your life in the future.

→ Consistency is key! It can take up to 66 repetitions to form a habit! We encourage you to think about what you have found helpful and to keep on doing it until it becomes a healthy, helpful habit.

→ You are more likely to be motivated to change your behaviour if the change is linked to something that has personal meaning and purpose and is important to you – we will talk a lot about using your Guide (Chapter 1) and your values to keep your life on track and moving forward in the way you want.

→ Mindfulness skills are effective for increasing awareness, improving focus, managing distress and appreciating the moment. We will show you some very brief, simple skills you can use every day that have known benefits.

→ Recording things by writing them down assists memory and helps build motivation – this is why we encourage you to use this book like a personal journal, and so that you can look back on what you have noted and see your own reminders.

Why is this book needed?

Research tells us that around 75% of mental health difficulties such as anxiety, low mood, lack of confidence and depression will first develop before a young person reaches their 18th birthday, and that many of these problems go on to remain a problem during adult life. Sadly, studies also show that only around a quarter of young people with problems such as depression will get the help that they need from professionals (Sadler *et al.* 2018; Mandalia *et al.* 2018; Evans-Lacko *et al.* 2018). Many young people have mental health problems that go unrecognised, and for others there may be difficulties with accessing support, due to long waiting times for mental health services that are increasingly stretched.

Even though emotional ups and downs happen to everyone, it's not always easy to talk about wellbeing and mental health. Some people find it easy to share how they are feeling with others, but you may also feel embarrassed or uncomfortable, and end up pulling away and becoming isolated just when you are most in need of understanding and friendship. Finding it hard to talk about how you are feeling can also get in the way of seeking help for mental health problems if needed, so it's important and helpful to learn how to talk about what's happening inside.

This book is designed to help you recognise how you are feeling early, before the feelings build up to become a major problem. The exercises and audio clips encourage you to use brief but effective skills and tools to help you cope with difficult feelings and to make a positive difference to your life and your future.

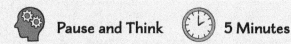

Pause and Think   5 Minutes

What brings you here?

What made you pick up this book and start reading? You have made a wise choice and a very important first step to get this far and have read up to here – even if you did it in short bursts and picked this book up and put it down again several times. Remember, do whatever works for you personally!

Life does not always run smoothly, and most of us are facing a wide range of different challenges and difficulties. When life is throwing up problems or complications, it often helps to give yourself a bit of brain space to think about yourself and how to deal with these issues on a regular basis. We find that spending a short time on a regular basis, perhaps on several days during the week, usually has the greatest benefit. This can create the space to think about exactly what you are struggling with and what you dream of or long for.

So, let's start by writing down a few concerns or difficulties you are having at the moment and what you would like to be different, even if you are not sure that you can make it happen right now:

The things that I am concerned about/struggling with are…

....

....

....

....

I would know that things were getting better if…

....

....

....

....

If things improved, then I would be able to...

....

....

....

....

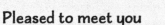 **Pause and Think** 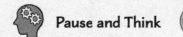 **5 Minutes**

Pleased to meet you

To know where we want to get to, it often helps to spend a short time thinking about who we are and where we have come from...

    Write a few descriptive words or sentences in or around the circles 'About you and your wider world'. You can add more later as you discover things about yourself as you go through this workbook.

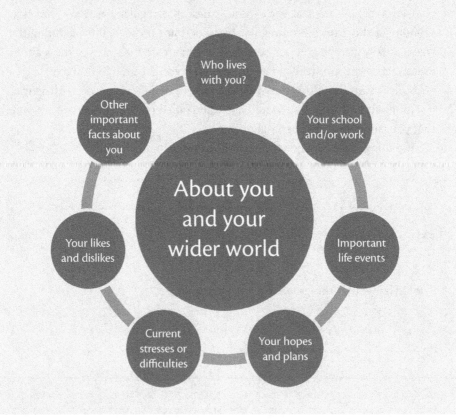

 **Read This** 🕐 **10 Minutes**

How do I use this book?

In this book we will introduce you to '10 Minute GROW'. This is a four-step set of life skills that can be learned and used in almost any situation, and it gives a framework for discovering what is helpful and works for you personally.

10 Minute GROW tools will help you take action and do things differently. We will encourage you to choose to do more things that take you **towards** what is important, and to notice and change behaviour that takes you **away** from what you care about or that keeps you feeling stuck or pushed around by unhelpful thoughts and feelings. This can help you learn to be more accepting of yourself and acts like a friendly coach, encouraging you towards a bright future.

This will all become clear as you work through the chapters of this book. And don't just read about it – to get the most out of the book we highly recommend that you complete the activities and try things out in practice too!

Many people find it helpful to go through the whole book to understand the approach in detail, but you can also dip in and out according to what seems most interesting or relevant to you.

However, we do recommend that you start by reading all four chapters in Part 1 before starting the rest of the book, as they provide all the important information needed to make the most of the approach.

We have also outlined some common difficulties encountered by young people and given examples of helpful ways of using 10 Minute GROW skills in different situations. You can ask your parents, teachers, friends and supporters to use these skills too and to help remind you to put them into practice. The QR codes throughout the book link to helpful video and audio clips. Please scan the code using the camera on your smartphone, open the tab and follow the prompts to register an account for the JKP Library. After you register, you can scan the code to access the content at any time, without having to give your details again.

Further reading and references are at the back of this book.

What is 10 Minute GROW?

So, what exactly is 10 Minute GROW? Here is a quick overview of the four steps that we'll be looking at in more detail throughout this book:

→ Step 1: Follow your **G**uide.

→ Step 2: Get **R**eady for Action.

→ Step 3: Be **O**pen and **O**bserve yourself and the world around you.

→ Step 4: Use your **Wise** Mind.

Let's briefly look at each of the four stages.

Follow your Guide

Your Guide acts like an inner compass and helps you choose which direction to take in life. It is about asking yourself: What do I care about? What kind of person do I want to be? What qualities do I want to encourage? What do I want out of life? Is what I am doing right now leading me in that direction? We will explore in more detail who and what are important to you – and whether you are living according to your most important values. This is a big ask, so don't expect to have all the answers at once! Think of it as an adventure – a journey of discovery.

Ready for Action

Being Ready for Action is a skill that involves behaving or doing things differently. You can choose to carry out small actions that lead you towards the people and the things that matter most. We can sometimes make decisions, set goals and take action quickly, if this will solve a problem or it is clear what needs to be done. At other times, you may be unsure what to do next, so you may need to experiment – try things out, try things on for size and see how they feel and if they fit with who you want to be. Being Ready for Action often involves taking small steps in the direction of what matters, without being certain what the outcome will be, and being willing to take your time in achieving important life goals.

Open and Observe

Being Open and able to Observe is an important step in understanding yourself and how you react to life experiences. This might involve tuning in to what you feel in your body and noticing your thoughts, feelings and urges to react in certain ways. Learning to be Open and Observe will allow you to stand back and take a moment to check how you are feeling and notice your inner reactions, without judging or criticising, and to acknowledge and make room for uncomfortable thoughts and feelings without getting caught up or overwhelmed by them. This helps create a space in which you can respond to different circumstances and make choices about which actions are most helpful for you.

Use your Wise Mind

Your 'mind' is the voice you hear in your head; your thoughts and beliefs; your stories. It has built up over time and is influenced by people and events in your life. This is part of your internal experiences – the parts that people do not see but that can affect what you do and how you react. Building a Wise Mind involves learning to notice your thoughts and ask yourself – are they helpful? Are they directing you towards your Guide and the things that matter most? We will learn skills to step back from unhelpful thoughts and pause before acting on impulse. We will also learn to build up our Wise Mind and to make helpful choices in how to act. We can also learn to tune out from unhelpful, negative and self-critical mind chattering that might be keeping you stuck and lacking in confidence and taking you away from your chosen direction in life.

 Watch This   **2 Minutes**

ALEX'S STORY

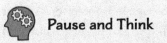 **Pause and Think**   **2 Minutes**

What is your instant reaction to the GROW model demonstrated by Alex's Story in the video? What questions do you have? Is there anything from the video that you could use?

....

....

....

What we have covered in the introduction

→ We introduced the concepts behind 10 Minute GROW and summarised the skills you will be learning in this book.

→ We suggested some tasks and encouraged you to listen, notice and record to reinforce your learning.

When you are ready, move on to Part 1, where we will look at each element of the 10 Minute GROW model in more detail.

The book continues with this format, taking you through the skills and applying them to difficulties that are common to young people. We hope you will continue on your journey of self-discovery.

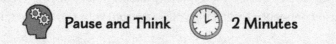 **Pause and Think** **2 Minutes**

Make a note of anything that you found particularly helpful, interesting or surprising so far.

....

....

....

What are you going to do next?

In the end, it's not what you read or watch or listen to, it's what you put into action that counts. Can you choose one small action for the coming week based on what you have read so far? Can you commit to reading this book and spending time on yourself for 10 minutes each day? Anything else?

Writing it down will help you remember. It will also help you to commit to doing something differently. Make a note of your thoughts here...

....

....

....

Part 1

INTRODUCING THE GROW FRAMEWORK AND STEPS TO BETTER MENTAL HEALTH

Chapter 1

FOLLOW YOUR GUIDE

→ Do you know who and what is important to you and have a clear direction for your life?

→ Do you find yourself going along with things that don't quite seem to fit with who you are, where you want to be or what you wish to do?

→ Do you ever take time to think about who and what you care most about in life?

It may help to explore and learn to use your Guide. Read on...

 Read This   5 Minutes

What is your Guide?

We each have our own individual and personal Guide. Your Guide is like an inner compass, pointing you in the direction of the people and things that are most important to **you** as a unique person.

Following your Guide involves:

→ keeping in mind who and what is important to you, and the things in life that you care about most

→ knowing your values – what makes you feel alive and gives your life meaning and purpose?

→ thinking about what qualities you wish to encourage and how you want to develop and grow as a person

→ taking action – doing things that take you in the direction you wish your life to go in.

The first step is to think about what you value and care about most in life and what kind of person you would like to become in the future. We will do this in this chapter by asking questions and completing some exercises.

 **Watch This** **2 Minutes**

FOLLOWING YOUR GUIDE VIDEO

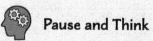 **Pause and Think** **5 Minutes**

You have become an instant billionaire – now what?!! (Spend a maximum of 3 minutes on this.)

Imagine you have become an instant billionaire and have only six months to use the money to do everything you want before your life changes again and the money is gone.

What would you do? Who would you do it with?

Make a note of your thoughts here:

....

....

....

....

....

....

Did what you wrote down surprise you?

What kinds of things are most important to you?

 **Read This** 🕐 **10 Minutes**

What are values?

Values are personal and not easy to define. They can be seen as important ideals that you hold and care about. A value is like a life direction, an internal compass that guides you throughout life.

Your values can affect the choices you make and the actions and behaviours that you carry out. They help to answer questions about why you might wish to take certain actions or make certain choices. They can also help you to decide how to do things, as well as what to do. This is the essence of knowing and using your Guide.

To identify your values, think about what is **really** important to you in life. What gives your life meaning and purpose? What motivates and drives what you do? How or what do you feel when you do important things?

Is it a sense of belonging that you get from spending time with your family or your friendship group? Does becoming football captain mean a lot to you because of ambition or because leadership is important to you? Does your love of creativity give you a sense of purpose when you make up a new tune or go to a pottery class? Perhaps your appreciation of nature makes you feel good when you spend time outdoors? Or does caring deeply about world matters mean that you campaign to make a difference in the world?

Why are values important?

Following your Guide and knowing your values is like having your own personal guiding star. It can help you to make decisions about what's important to you and can help you to create a life that has meaning and purpose, allowing you to behave in a way that 'fits' with who you want to be as a person. When you are truly Following your Guide, you will be more aware and more in control. You will make active choices about what you are doing rather than just reacting to things on autopilot, being stuck in a rut doing what you have always done or following what others around you are doing, without being happy with where you are heading.

Finding your values can also help to create an anchor that keeps you stable through the ups and downs and the busy chaos of daily life. Following your Guide towards your values will help you to bring energy and attention to important issues that are part of the big picture of what matters to you in life, whatever that might be. Ultimately, Following your Guide feels right and can give a sense of purpose that will help you to cope with stress and improve your wellbeing and mood.

APPLYING THE SKILLS IN ACTION

Tom cares passionately about nature and the environment. He takes part in local conservation projects and rallies regarding global warming, and he is studying geography and ecology. Keeping healthy and in good shape is also important to him, and he is training for a marathon. He also cares about his friend Sam, who has recently had an injury. Tom also loves listening to music.

Tom runs round the park regularly and knows he needs to look after his body by keeping hydrated and drinking plenty of water. He chooses to bring a refillable bottle of water with him rather than buy multiple plastic ones like other joggers. He travels to college by bike or by bus rather than driving, to reduce emissions into the environment. Every week, Tom does exercise with Sam by doing a slower walk/jog routine to help him recover from his injury. Tom often goes to watch bands at the weekend and shares his favourite music playlists with a wider group of friends.

The reasons why Tom chooses certain actions can be understood by knowing who and what is important to him and what he cares about. Tom's actions are in line with his values and the kind of person he wants to be.

Can you pick out **who** and **what** is important to Tom? Why does he choose certain actions? How does he act in line with his values?

....

....

....

Read This   10 Minutes

Values versus goals and actions

It helps to think of values as a broad direction rather than a defined goal or target to be ticked off a 'to-do' list. For example, your value might be friendship or connection rather than spending time with one specific person, or it might be education and learning rather than achieving a specific qualification.

As you get to know your values and Follow your Guide, you will understand more about where you want to go in life, allowing you to set goals and choose specific actions that are in line with your most important values. We call this taking a step **towards** your values. For example, you might choose to spend time with a close friend or go for a walk in nature rather than watching TV at the weekend. We will learn more about choosing actions and setting goals in Chapter 2.

Values are...	Values are not...
✓ Directions you choose: The journey and the route that you travel, not the destination or outcome.	✘ Goals that you can achieve, milestones you can reach or things you can tick off on a 'to-do' list.
✓ Freely chosen by each individual person; they may be similar, overlapping or completely different from the people around you or in your culture.	✘ Following someone else's rules or ideas about what is important without taking your own ideas into account.
✓ Long-standing but flexible patterns of activity that can change over time or change in importance, according to circumstances.	✘ It's not always necessary to please other people or to fit in, so following your values may therefore not always feel comfortable – at least in the short term.
✓ A good fit with the kind of person you want to be and the personal qualities you wish to develop over your lifetime.	✘ There are no fixed and rigid answers or rules to be followed at all times regardless of the circumstances, situations or your age.
✓ The big picture: Thinking beyond just yourself and seeing different ways to achieve your values.	✘ Focusing only on yourself or on one specific goal.

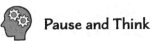 Pause and Think  10 Minutes

Finding your values: what things matter to you?

Sometimes, it may be difficult to define your values, or even to decide whether you are conforming to other people's values rather than your own. Asking yourself some questions can help you to learn more about your own values.

Parvin says that 'work' and 'getting a good job' are important to her. But are these values, life areas or goals?

Work is a life area that is important to her. Getting a job is the outcome she wants — a goal — rather than the value.

So, what is her value? To find this out, we could begin by asking Parvin what she means by a 'good job'. This might help to identify her reasons for this goal and the values that lie beneath it.

Parvin says that she sees a 'good job' as being one that she enjoys and has the opportunities for future promotion, even if this doesn't happen right away. She would be happy to carry on studying and learning if this would help her to make progress in the future. Parvin is good with numbers and enjoys maths. She thinks that she might like to use these interests and skills in the workplace. She also likes working with other people and would like to be part of a team in an office. She would like to earn enough money to eventually move out from her parents' home and live independently.

Given this information, underline what Parvin's most important values might be in the life area of work (choose up to three):

Achievement – Ambition – Belonging – Challenge – Learning – Independence – Individuality – Wealth – Anything else?

If you are not sure, what else could you ask her to find out what motivates her the most?

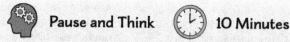

Pause and Think   **10 Minutes**

What are your values (right now)?

Below is a chart that shows some possible values and some blank spaces so that you can add anything important that is missing.

Consider each value. Place a cross (✖) next to that value if it's not important to you at all. Place one (✓), two (✓ ✓) or three ticks (✓ ✓ ✓) to show whether it is a little important, fairly important or very important to you at the moment. Add any important values that you think are missing from the list.

Value	How important? ✖ ✓ ✓ ✓	Value	How important? ✖ ✓ ✓ ✓
Achievement: Setting goals and working towards important accomplishments.		**Individuality:** Exploring and experimenting with being the unique person you wish to be.	
Adventure: Having new and exciting experiences.		**Leadership:** Taking charge and having responsibility for guiding others.	
Ambition: Having drive, thinking about the future and expanding your opportunities.		**Learning and education:** Expanding knowledge and skills or having specialist knowledge about an interest.	

Being active: Participating in physical activities, dance or sports.	**Connection:** Finding and expressing love, closeness and affection with others.
Belonging: Being part of a community, group, organisation or culture or participating in family life.	**Nature:** The outdoors, animals and the natural world.
Body: Caring for your health, body and appearance.	**Order:** Being organised, following or developing a pattern or routine.
Challenge: Solving problems, stretching your limits and testing your abilities.	**World matters:** Politics or global or environmental issues.
Creativity: Expressing and appreciating creativity, such as music and art.	**Safety:** Finding physical and emotional safety, security and trust in yourself and others.
Fun: Humour, laughter and enjoyment.	**Spirituality and religion:** Upholding personal beliefs, traditions and practices.
Giving: Supporting, caring and encouraging others or the wider community.	**Wealth:** Having money to spend as you choose.
Other: Is anything else important?	

 **Read This**   **5 Minutes**

Who do you want to be?
Finding a life purpose

Looking for purpose and meaning in life is about looking beyond yourself and developing your desire to make a difference in the world and contribute to things that are bigger than you. Research suggests that finding a sense of purpose can lead to improvements in optimism, help people to cope better with setbacks and life problems and build brighter expectations about the future (Ho, Cheung and Cheung 2010). Finding a life purpose might involve:

→ getting motivated and finding ways to get more involved with topics or subjects that you are interested in

→ seeking out and engaging in values that relate to a sense of meaning or purpose

→ looking at the big picture and being open to learning more about different perspectives and alternative ways of looking at the world

→ finding ways to contribute to your local communities and to the wider world

→ thinking about what bothers, worries or upsets you about the world, and what tiny steps you could take that might make a small difference.

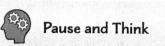 **Pause and Think** **5 Minutes**

Superhero exercise

There are many ways to improve our world – but which ones do you care about most? Imagine that you are given three superpowers for just one week. They can only be used to make some kind of improvement in the world. Which superpowers would you choose? Would you choose super-strength, telekinesis, mind reading... or something else? How would you use your powers to make the world better?

Back to real life! What tiny steps could you make that would take an action that might also lead to an improvement in the world? Don't worry about how big the steps are or what the final outcome is, just think about moving in the direction of what's important...

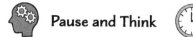 **Pause and Think**  **5 Minutes**

Values and personal qualities

Acknowledging and developing your personal qualities can be an important part of living according to your values. Qualities such as patience, kindness, honesty and reliability can move you towards values such as relationships and connection with others. We will think more about important personal qualities in Chapter 8.

Sally is a sociable girl who likes to have fun with her friends and go out to parties. She likes to live life at a fast pace and finds it difficult to slow down. When she is out with friends she likes to dance, chat to lots of different people and move from one venue to another to see as many of her friends as possible during the evening.

Sally has a close relationship with her grandad, who is very important to her. As he has grown older, he has developed problems with his memory and has become much slower at moving than before. Sally sometimes finds it hard to be patient but she cares for her grandad a great deal, so when she visits him, she deliberately slows down, repeats things and stays with him for several hours, looking at the newspaper on a Saturday afternoon.

Sally encourages the quality of patience in herself in order to bring her value of caring for her grandad to life.

What personal qualities might be important for your own values?

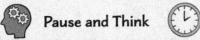 **Pause and Think** **10 Minutes**

Pick your values (for now)

Go back to the list of values on page 22. Choose four to eight of your **most important** values (for now) and place a star by them. Remember, this is a work in progress, so you can change or update these at any stage if you need to. You have a right to change your mind, to experiment and to try different values on for size to see which suit you best. Write them down here:

....

....

....

Once you have your list, ask yourself these questions.

→ How easy or difficult was it to pick the most important values?

→ Did any surprise you?

→ Are they balanced? Is there a combination of fun and responsibility? Is it all pleasure and no substance? Or all work and no fun? Are they satisfying and sustainable?

→ Are there any important values that are missing or that you have neglected for a while?

➜ Are there any values that conflict with each other, the people around you or the circumstances you are in?

➜ Are there any values that you are holding too tightly and are becoming a pressure or demand?

➜ Would it help to be more flexible or hold some values more loosely, so that you can prioritise what is most important for now? For example, being sociable with friends is important, but achievement might be more important during exam periods. You can still hold both values but the priority you give each one might vary.

Make a note of your thoughts here:

. . . .

. . . .

. . . .

 Pause and Think 🕐 **10 Minutes**

Bringing values to life

Now that you have chosen some of your most important values, the next step is to bring them to life by taking action and starting to live according to them. This involves making decisions and taking steps in the direction that your Guide is pointing you towards. It is important to be flexible and seek different and varied ways of acting out values across different areas of your life.

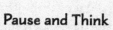

We will think a lot more about how to choose actions to bring your values to life in Chapter 2. For now, ask yourself these questions.

→ How closely are you living according to your values? How close are you to 'hitting the bullseye' in each area of your life?

→ What are you doing to achieve this? What personal qualities can you encourage in order to move towards the bullseye?

→ What area(s) of life are you doing better in and which area(s) needs attention?

→ Are you getting the right kind of balance, or do you need to make any changes to give more attention to certain aspects of life?

In Chapter 2, we will look in more detail at goals that are in keeping with your values and small actions you can take that would take you a step towards the bullseye. Can you think of one for now? Write it here: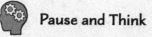

....

....

....

....

....

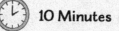 **Pause and Think**   🕐 **10 Minutes**

Troubleshooting values...
What if I'm still not sure what my values are?
It's normal and common to not feel sure about what your values are, and your priorities might change at different points in your life. This is an ongoing process, and you may need to revisit them several times!

Here are some questions that might help you to clarify your values. Make a note of your ideas and answers here.

What qualities do you have that you can acknowledge?

....

....

....

Who inspires you?

....

....

....

Who do you look up to? What is it about their vision, skills or personal qualities that you admire?

....

....

....

Sometimes, it helps to ask for feedback from other people. Try asking one or more people that you trust:

→ What do you think I'm good at?

→ What are my greatest strengths?

→ What do you think I really enjoy doing?

→ When do you think I'm most focused or interested in what I'm doing?

→ How do you think I'll leave my mark on the world?

I'm interested in lots of values – I don't know which ones to choose!

You might have an interest in many different values and find it hard to narrow down which ones are most important. That's fine too. Sometimes, it's important to keep an open mind to allow yourself to change and develop, and to not decide what to focus on too early without considering other ideas.

Try them on for size! If you are finding it hard to narrow down your ideas about values, you could just choose a set of values that you are interested in right now and try them out to see how they fit in your life. You could experiment with choosing some actions relating to these values and see how that feels and what effect it has on your life. Make sure to come back to the values section in this chapter regularly and make any changes that you need to as you develop your identity, roles, interests and personal qualities.

Which values make a good starting point for your life right now? Which ones can you experiment with? Remember, you can always adapt these as your life develops and changes!

....

....

I'm feeling overwhelmed – these choices seem so big and I'm not sure how to get started!

Don't worry – you don't have to start by making big changes, even if the problems that you care about are important issues. Instead, you can start small and look for **sparks**. These are tiny glimmers of light that shine in the direction of your values. We will think more about ways to make tiny or micro-steps in the direction of your values in Chapter 2.

What tiny **sparks** or micro-steps might move you towards one or more of your important values?

....

....

....

I feel alone – no one shares my values

Your values are your own unique perspective on the world, although they may be shaped by your experiences and your culture. But it can be an isolating and lonely experience to feel that you are alone and that there is no one who understands or shares some of your most important or personal values.

It can help to actively seek out others who do share your values – to find a tribe or a community of people who will understand your perspective and who might support you in taking action in line with these values, even if the actions might sometimes involve hard work or other challenges. Finding just one other person who shares a value might be enough, or you may find a whole community to offer support and encouragement. This could be face to face or via an online or virtual group.

Talking about your values with others will help to bring them to life and may even create a spark of interest that encourages other people with a similar value to take action. We talk more about ways to connect with others in Chapter 9.

How could you find ways to connect with others who might share some of your important values?

....

....

....

....

....

My values are conflicting or getting in the way of each other! What should I do?

Naomi values spending time with her friends, and she also cares about her family and her schoolwork. Sometimes, she feels that these different values are in competition with each other and it's hard to know what to choose to do, especially when her parents complain that she doesn't spend enough time with them! Are her values in conflict? What should she do?

The first thing to remember is that values are not the same as specific goals or actions. Values are broad aspects of life that are important to you. It is possible to hold different values at the same time – Naomi can value her friends **and** her family **and** her schoolwork. It is the ways that we choose to act out a value, and how much time and energy we choose to put into different activities, that might sometimes conflict. But it is also possible to find flexible solutions that address all her different values. Perhaps she has breakfast with her parents, studies for a few hours and then meets a friend for a break at lunchtime.

There are many ways to act out your values and one of the key skills is to be flexible, be creative and look for solutions that work well in your life. You may need to experiment on different days or weeks to find out what works best for you. Remember, there is no 'correct' or 'perfect' solution – it's usually a question of deciding what to try and seeing what happens.

Does it ever feel like some of your different values are in conflict? Which ones? Can you think of any creative solutions that allow you to care about all your different values?

....

....

....

....

....

 Pause and Think **10 Minutes**

Notice when you are using your Guide

Think about a recent time when you felt alive and in tune with who you want to be – doing the things you want to do and feeling that there was meaning and purpose to life. It may help to pick a photo on your phone to remind you and use the following questions to help you describe the event or moment fully.

What were you doing? When was this? Where? Who with? Describe the situation using your five senses to bring it alive.	
What did you feel in your body? What emotion came up?	
What value(s) did this event link to?	
How do you feel now, thinking about it again? What action might you take?	

What we have covered in Chapter 1: Using your Guide

→ Using your Guide is like following a guiding star that will help you find your life direction and feel good about yourself.

→ Discovering which values are most important to you at the moment involves asking yourself questions such as:

> Who is important to me? What is important? What kind of person do I wish to be? What gives my life meaning and purpose?

→ Values are not goals and cannot be 'ticked off' on a to-do list.

→ It is important for values to be balanced, adaptable and not rigid; they may change with time as you grow and develop.

→ **How** you do things is also part of using your Guide – this involves encouraging yourself to act in line with your qualities and becoming the person you wish to be.

→ So, now you have explored your values and priorities, let's Use your Guide!

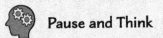 **Pause and Think** **5 Minutes**

→ What are the most important messages for you from this chapter?

→ What have you learned or understood after reading it and trying the exercises?

→ What are you going to do differently now?

→ What actions will you take after reading this chapter?

→ Are there any values you are thinking about differently or qualities you are going to encourage?

....
....
....
....

Chapter 2

READY FOR ACTION

→ Do you ever find yourself saying, 'I'll do that tomorrow because I can't be bothered now,' and then not doing it at all?

→ Do you worry about whether you will be able to do things well enough and then avoid doing them altogether?

→ Do you feel overwhelmed by an ever-growing to-do list, pressured, like you're underachieving or 'nagged at' by others?

→ Do you want to feel Ready for Action? Read on...

 **Read This** 🕐 **10 Minutes**

Get Ready to take Action!

Taking action means doing the things that are most important to you. This can be one of the simplest yet most effective ways of dealing with problems and creating a positive and fulfilling life.

In the previous chapter, we looked at your Guide and finding out what you value and care about most in life. The next step is to start to **act out** some of these values, moving from ideas to concrete actions in your life.

Trying out new ways of behaving or reacting can create an opportunity for positive things to happen and to get important things done. It's often far easier to change your actions than your attitudes or beliefs. And you can make changes in very small steps that are realistic, meaningful and achievable.

Taking action involves:

→ trying something new rather than staying stuck in old habits or patterns of behaviour that are no longer working

→ doing things because they are important even when your mind might be telling you that there's no point, or it feels uncomfortable

→ focusing on the actions that matter most to you

→ taking time to think about what small actions might make a big impact in your life.

What is an action?

When we talk about actions, we are really talking about behaviour or what we do. Behaviour usually involves a physical action that can be seen, felt, heard or touched. Someone watching you would be able to observe and describe what actions you are carrying out: you might sit down, look at your phone, go for a walk or buy a sandwich for lunch. These are all types of **external** actions (outside the mind).

You might also carry out **internal** actions, which take place within your mind. Internal actions tend to involve thinking about something repeatedly, such as getting caught up in worries or mentally planning for the future.

Your actions can have a big impact on your mood. Some actions, such as spending time with a close friend, can lift your mood and make you feel upbeat and positive. Other actions can make you feel isolated, low and more prone to worry. It can be helpful to take some time to notice whether a particular action is adding value and positivity to your life – is it enjoyable, important or uplifting? Or is it acting as a 'life-drain' – sucking up your time and making you feel more negative, fed up or lacking in energy or confidence?

Most people's actions tend to follow repeated patterns or habits. You might not even think about this or notice how often you are carrying them out. But getting stuck in the habit of repeated negative or unhelpful actions can lead to all kinds of difficulties and emotional distress.

The good news is that you don't have to stick with old habits if they are no longer working. You can choose your actions and can use this choice to take control of the direction of your life.

Life-boosting actions:

→ are enjoyable and uplifting

→ give you a sense of achievement or satisfaction

→ are important or meaningful to you.

Life-draining actions:

→ lower your mood or energy

→ don't add value to your life

→ involve avoiding or putting off doing things that are important.

 **Watch This**  **2 Minutes**

READY FOR ACTION VIDEO

Pause and Think ⏱ **10 Minutes**

Noticing your own actions

Think about a time within the past day or so when you had some free time. Make a list of the actions that you carried out. Make the list as long as possible. Try to include very small actions, such as filling up a water bottle, as well as bigger actions, such as going out to meet a friend. Think about how long each action lasted and decide, on balance, whether each activity was life-boosting or life-draining.

What was the action?	How long did you do it for?	Life-boosting (LB) or life-draining (LD)?

 Read This  5 Minutes

Moving from values to actions

You will be more motivated and likely to do something if it has meaning to you person-ally and is a good 'fit' with who you are. This means taking time to actively choose actions that are in line with your values and using your Guide to help decide what these are.

Your values are like the roots of a tree. They provide the support, strength and stability that enable the tree to grow strong and healthy.

From your values come your goals and plans for the future. These are the branches of the tree stretching upwards and out-wards in many different directions. What direction will you choose to take your life in? They might include smaller twigs, such as plans for the next day or week, as well as larger branches, which repre-sent long-terms plans for the next months or even years.

And finally, there are individual tiny actions that create the overall shape and beauty of the tree. These are the hundreds or even thousands of leaves that all together provide the tree with energy to develop and grow.

 Pause and Think  5 Minutes

Go back to the list of things you spend your time on that you just made and ask your-self the following questions:

→ Is each action **in line** with your values?

→ What are you doing that is a good 'fit' with who you want to be? Put a tick against these actions or activities.

Values, goals and actions

→ **Values** involve listening to your Guide and deciding what is most important to you.

→ **Goals and plans** involve thinking about what you would like to achieve in the future.

→ **Actions** involve taking small steps to carry out specific activities and behaviours.

 Read This  5 Minutes

Seeking adventure: explore and discover

One of the important steps in being Ready for Action is to seek out new adventures and to be willing to explore and discover new ways of living. This means experimenting and trying new ways of doing things, even though you may not be sure what will happen. This can be a little uncomfortable at first, because old habits can feel safe and secure, even if they are not really very healthy or positive. But by taking steps into the unknown, you can start to build new habits that are more closely linked to your values.

You can bring a sense of adventure when choosing your actions by looking for new activities to try or by finding new ways to do tasks that you already carry out. Like all great adventures, this might sometimes be a little uncomfortable, but it can also lead you in all kinds of new and exciting directions.

Rob values fitness but has recently become a bit bored with his usual swimming sessions and has stopped going to the pool regularly. He's noticed that he's started gaining weight and is feeling more sluggish. He decides to experiment with being more adventurous and to try something new. He combines his values of nature with fitness, friendship and caring for the environment to plan some new energy-boosting actions.

Pick one of your important values	List some activities that link to this value	Pick one activity – can you plan some small steps for trying this?
Fitness and outdoors	Join a running group that meets for a Sunday park jog.	Look on the internet for how to register. Talk to Rupal who already goes and arrange to meet her there.
Friendship	Get back into playing football.	Text Paul and Jenna to see who is free to play tomorrow. Offer to play with my neighbour's son who loves football.
Caring for others	Helping my gran as she has a bad knee. Help my friends when they need it.	Take Gran's dog out for a walk at the weekend. Spend 15 minutes helping Jim with his maths homework.
Nature and environment	Help with local conservation.	Talk to Amit who volunteers on the pond clearance project. To reduce waste, stop using plastic straws and ask my friends to do the same.

Pause and Think 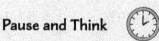 **5 Minutes**

Now it's your turn to plan some actions that are related to your most important values. In the following chart, make a list of some of the most important values that you found in Chapter 1. Try to bring in a spirit of discovery and adventure by thinking about new things to try or new ways to do things that you already do.

In the next column, brainstorm a list of activities that might be linked to this value. At this stage, don't worry too much about whether these are practical or realistic. Just write down as many ideas as you can think of. Try to be creative and include things that you have never tried. You could also ask someone for help with generating new ideas.

Choose one of the activities and break it into small, achievable actions that you could try in the next few days.

Pick one of your important values	List some activities that link to this value	Pick one activity – can you plan some small steps for trying this?

 **Do This** **10 Minutes**

Choose some actions to try

The next step is to pick some actions to carry out. Choose one to three activities from your previous brainstorming session that you can carry out within the next few days. For each action, ask yourself these questions.

→ What am I going to do?

→ Which value is this linked to?

→ Where am I going to do it?

→ When am I going to do it?

→ Who am I going to do it with?

→ For how long and how often am I going to do it?

Finish by asking yourself: how likely is it that I will do this (from 1 to 10)?

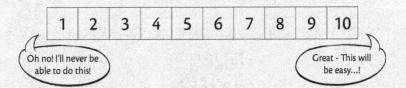

Aim for a confidence level of **8, 9 or 10** that you will carry out this action. If you are feeling any less confident, try changing your planned action to make it more achievable. Think: What would make this easier to carry out? Can you make it into a smaller step? Can you ask someone for help?

For each action complete the next chart. Here are some of Rob's answers:

What am I going to do?	I'm going to walk my gran's dog.
Which value is this linked to?	Being outdoors, animals, caring for others.
Where am I going to do it?	Round the local park.
When am I going to do it?	On Sunday morning straight after breakfast.
Who am I going to do it with?	My friend Sara.
For how long/how often am I going to do it?	Half an hour.
How likely is it that I will do this (from 1 to 10)? What might get in the way? How could I make this easier to carry out? Aim for at least 8–10 likelihood that you will carry out this action!	8/10 If it rains or if Sara doesn't come, I might not want to bother, so I will just go for 10 minutes.

Now it's your turn...

What am I going to do?

Which value is this linked to?

Where am I going to do it?

When am I going to do it?

Who am I going to do it with?

For how long/how often am I going to do it?

How likely is it that I will do this (from 1 to 10)? What might get in the way?
How could I make this easier to carry out?
Aim for at least 8–10 likelihood that you will carry out this action!

You can download more blank tables from

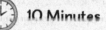 Pause and Think 10 Minutes

What happened when you tried the action?

After you try out an action, take a few minutes to think about what happened, so that you can give yourself a pat on the back for anything that went well and learn from anything that might not have gone according to plan. Fill out the following chart.

What had you planned to do? What did you try?

Was this action linked to any of your important values?

What was the short-term impact of
doing this?

What might be the long-term impact?

What can you learn from this?

How can you build on this? What will
you try next (different or the same)?

If the action didn't quite go according to plan, there are some other helpful
questions to think about. Ask yourself these questions.

What got in the way? E.g. I ran out of
time, I forgot, it was too difficult or
something else important came up...

Is this still something important to
you? If not, what else could you try?

What could make it easier next time?
Can you break it into a smaller step?
How can you remember to try it?

Here are Rob's answers after he walked his gran's dog:

*Sara didn't want to come as she had too much homework, but it wasn't raining
so I went anyway. I took the dog out for about 10 minutes and then came back
because I felt a bit silly on my own. Then I felt bad because he still had lots of
energy and kept barking! But Gran was pleased to see me and at least I tried. Next
time, I'll try to go for a bit longer, even if Sara can't make it again. If it rains, I'll just
wear a coat and brave it on my own.*

 **Read This** 🕐 **5 Minutes**

What gets in the way? Towards Actions and Away Actions

Even though we may have the best intentions, it can sometimes be very hard to carry out actions that take us towards our values. We can get stuck in a negative pattern, where we take the same actions over and over again, even when they are not helping us to move towards an important area of our lives. Why is this?

When faced with challenging situations, people often get caught up in distressing thoughts, emotions and body sensations and have a strong urge to try to reduce this discomfort. In the example of walking the dog in the park, Rob came back early because he felt 'silly on his own'. He responded to his internal unhelpful thought and his uncomfortable feeling, and left early, much to the unhappiness of the dog. This action took him **away** from his value of caring for others.

In another example, Anna goes to a party and starts to feel anxious about talking to new people, so she decides to go home again. This temporarily reduces her anxiety, but it moves her away from her values of friendship and social connection.

Rob and Anna both show examples of Away Actions. These are actions that aim to reducing difficult feelings or distress but pull us away from what is important in the long term: the people and things that matter most to us. Alternatively, we can carry out actions that are in line with our values and fit with who we want to be, taking us **towards** who and what matters. Often, this will make us feel satisfied and create a sense of enjoyment and control over life.

Sometimes, we may need to take a Towards Action even when this might involve a bit of discomfort. Perhaps we accept that we may feel a little nervous beforehand to be able to participate in a performance or a show, or we make the hard choice to study for an important test rather than playing a computer game we enjoy. By allowing the uncomfortable feelings to be there, we are able to carry out a Towards Action, which moves us towards something important. This may not be easy! You will learn more skills for how to do this as we progress through the book.

Towards and Away Actions

Towards Actions involve taking steps that bring you closer to the people and experiences that are most important to you.

Away Actions pull you away from the things that matter. They are usually carried out to try to get rid of a difficult thought, feeling or body sensation.

Pause and Think   **5 Minutes**

Take a look at the following examples of Away Actions. Do you ever carry out any of these? Put a tick next to the ones that you recognise. What other Away Actions do you sometimes do?

Examples of Away Actions

→ Not trying so that you can't fail.

→ Not asking for help when you need it.

→ Putting off doing something important because you feel fed up.

→ Underestimating your ability or listening to unhelpful and negative thoughts and feelings, such as fear and self-doubt.

→ Being too demanding of yourself and having too high expectations and un-realistic goals.

→ Not being assertive or expressing your own opinion or needs to others.

→ Getting caught up in activities that drain your time and not making time for the things that matter.

→ Spending time with people or in places that make it harder to do something important.

Make a note of some of your own examples of Away Actions here:

....

....

....

....

....

....

....

....

 Read This 10 Minutes

More about Towards Actions and Away Actions

Look at the following diagram. Remember, there is no 'right' or 'wrong' choice of action. What's important is whether, in this specific situation, an action is moving you **towards** or **away** from the things that matter most to you.

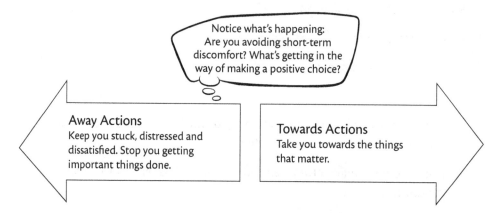

Let's think about an example of completing a difficult assignment or project. How might this involve Towards Actions and Away Actions?

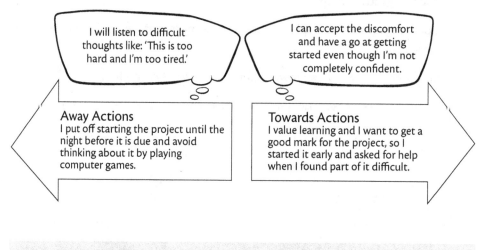

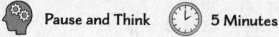 Pause and Think 5 Minutes

Think about something that you would really like to do more of but are finding difficult. What's getting in the way? Consider your own example and write your answers in the spaces in the following diagram.

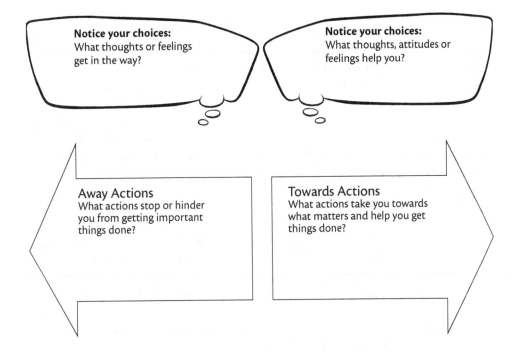

Notice your choices:
What thoughts or feelings get in the way?

Notice your choices:
What thoughts, attitudes or feelings help you?

Away Actions
What actions stop or hinder you from getting important things done?

Towards Actions
What actions take you towards what matters and help you get things done?

Being ready: myths, facts and towards action remedies

 Read This 10 Minutes

Myth	Fact	Towards Action
I have to be motivated and be in the right mood before I can get started.	Motivation only comes through doing something and then getting feedback. In a 'snowball effect', you gain motivation and momentum as you get the positive feedback of getting started.	✓ Behave as if you feel brighter or more motivated and the feeling will catch up. ✓ Take one small step towards getting started. ✓ Experiment and see what happens.
I'm too tired to start. I need to rest and save my energy.	Tiredness and lethargy improve with gradually increasing activity, not rest. The more you do, the more energy you will gain as you grow stronger and fitter.	✓ Break the task down so it seems less overwhelming. ✓ Start low, go slow and build up. ✓ Just do it and the feeling will catch up.

cont.

Myth	Fact	Towards Action
There isn't enough time to get important things done.	Try to prioritise and make sure that you do the most important tasks first.	✓ Think: What is essential to achieve today? ✓ Do priority tasks first, even if they are least enjoyable. ✓ Plan small, realistic actions rather than attempting too much.
If I hate the task or find it difficult, I can't do it, even if it's important.	We all need to do things we don't enjoy sometimes in order to achieve long-term goals and avoid negative consequences. This may involve short-term discomfort or considerable effort. Take a breath and go for it! We will look at coping with difficult feelings in the next chapter.	✓ Visualise how satisfied you will feel when it's completed. ✓ Relate it to your values: Is this important for me or someone else I care about? ✓ Ask for help: Share the load or find a task buddy or supporter. ✓ Try a countdown to action: Breathe in and then breathe out: 3... 2... 1... GO.
The things I want are impossible. There's no point even trying to achieve them.	Few things are impossible, but you may need to adjust your goals. Just take a tiny step – don't expect a leap! We will learn more about facing and overcoming challenges in Chapter 11.	✓ Adjust your goals if necessary. ✓ Upskill yourself or ask for help. ✓ Get prepared – have the right tools and equipment ready in advance. ✓ Keep practising and acknowledge your efforts.

Pause and Think   5 Minutes

→ Which of the above 'myths' have stopped you from doing things?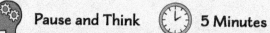

→ Which of the Towards Action remedies can you try?

. . . .

. . . .

. . . .

What we have covered in Chapter 2: Ready for Action

→ Your actions can affect how you think and feel about yourself and your life.

→ You can choose your actions. It is the sum of all our actions that creates the patterns of our lives.

→ Actions are more likely to be enjoyable, nourishing and life-boosting if they are in line with your values and the person you want to be (Towards Actions).

→ Choosing specific, important and achievable goals can help motivate you to make important changes.

→ Taking Towards Actions may be a bit uncomfortable at first, but it is worth exploring and discovering new ways of living your life that fit with what you care about.

→ There are many common myths that can keep you from finding the courage to give a new action a try. You now know the facts and some ways to beat the myths!

→ Making positive choices can lead to longer-term gains and help you break free from unhelpful patterns that might be keeping you stuck.

→ Now... pick an action and try it out. This chapter is about taking action and not just talking about it... use your Guide and be Ready for Action!

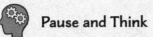 **Pause and Think** **5 Minutes**

→ What are the most important messages for you from this chapter?

→ What have you learned or understood after reading it and trying the exercises?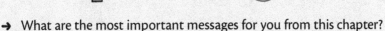

....

....

....

Taking action

→ What are you going to do differently now?

→ What actions will you take as a result of reading this chapter?

➜ Are there any regular actions or patterns of behaviour that you might try to practise or develop?

....

....

....

Chapter 3

OPEN AND OBSERVE

→ Do you sometimes find it hard to make sense of your emotions or just want to be rid of those difficult thoughts and feelings?

→ Do you find it easy to concentrate or does your attention wander, leaving you confused or uncertain about what to do next?

→ Do you ever find yourself stuck in regrets about the past or fears about the future?

→ Have you got 10 minutes to notice what's happening in your mind or body? Read on...

Be Open and Observe within

This chapter is about learning to be more aware of what's happening inside you – to recognise your inner reactions and to make sense of what you are going through. This is a useful skill that can help you to understand yourself, cope under pressure and step back and 'observe' rather than react instantly. This gives you more choice about what to do next.

In this fast-paced digital age, you are facing more pressures and worries than any generation that came before you. Open and Observing skills can help you notice what is going on inside your mind, inside your body and in the world around you and still choose to do what matters.

So, in this next chapter, you will learn to:

→ notice what's happening in the here and now, in your body and mind or in the environment around you

→ recognise your thoughts and feelings without judging them or getting caught up and reacting to them

→ continue to Follow your Guide and do things that take you towards your values, even when difficult thoughts and feelings show up.

▶ Watch This   🕐 2 Minutes

OPEN AND OBSERVING VIDEO

🧠 Pause and Think   🕐 2 Minutes

What was your instant reaction to the video? How might being Open and Observing help you? What might be difficult about it?

....

....

....

....

📖 Read This   🕐 5 Minutes

Noticing the now

Have you ever arrived somewhere and had no memory about what you saw on the way or even what route you took to get there?

Or have you ever walked straight past someone without even noticing them because your mind was too busy going over the disagreement you just had with your friend?

We can think of this as being on 'automatic pilot'. You do things but without really paying attention to what's happening right now. Instead, your mind is elsewhere – going over something that happened in the past or planning, worrying or dreaming about something that might happen in the future.

One of the first Open and Observe skills involves learning to come back out of your daydreams and 'notice the now'. But what exactly does this mean? It simply means instead of drifting in your mind's stories, you are awake, noticing and watching what's happening right at this moment. This is the first part of learning to Observe yourself and your own reactions to whatever situations you are facing. This can help you to appreciate and enjoy the positive moments in life, and to be more aware of life's challenges without getting overwhelmed by them.

 **Try This** 🕐 **30 Seconds**

Clap your hands – 30-second mindfulness: Close your eyes and hold your hands out in front of you. Clap your hands together and listen to the sound. Repeat the clap three times slowly and play close attention to what you feel in your hands and fingers.

Congratulations! You have been present in the moment!

Make a note of what you noticed here:

. . . .

. . . .

. . . .

. . . .

Alternatives to clapping: Rub your hands vigorously for a few seconds or squeeze and clench your hands into fists a few times. Now pause and pay close attention to how your fingers and hands feel.

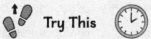 **Try This** 🕐 **3 Minutes**

Notice this moment

Stop whatever you are doing for a few seconds and notice what your senses are experiencing. Answer these questions:

→ What sounds can you hear?

→ What can you smell or taste (if anything)?

➜ What are you touching with your hands or any part of your skin?

➜ Are there any sensations inside your body – fluttering, warmth, aching, softness, tightness…?

Finish by taking one long, slow breath.
    Now write down what you noticed:
Around you (outside your body):

. . . .

. . . .

. . . .

Inside your body:

. . . .

. . . .

. . . .

Did notice any feelings or emotions?

. . . .

. . . .

. . . .

Was anything uncomfortable?

. . . .

. . . .

. . . .

What went through your mind (thoughts, memories, images)?

. . . .

. . . .

. . . .

 Read This  5 Minutes

Being more mindful...

Being Open and Observing is also known as mindfulness. Research shows that practising mindfulness helps to reduce distress, improve focus and allow you to appreciate life more (Halliwell 2010). But don't worry, it doesn't have to take a lot of time. Just a few minutes each day can help you to feel more aware and better able to cope with difficult thoughts and feelings.

You might have heard about mindfulness or tried it already. And even if you've never heard about it, the good news is that you already know how to do it!

Think about those amazing moments in life when you **really** noticed what was going on around you. For example, have you ever:

→ hung out with some good friends and found that the time just flew by because you were having such a great time

→ watched an amazing sunset or a beautiful view and felt that it was a magical experience

→ got so involved in an activity or a sport that you were 'in the zone' and it just felt natural to keep going

→ listened to a song and felt your emotions soar with the music

→ stroked a pet and felt calm, peaceful and connected to the animal?

All these activities involve being aware of what's happening at that moment – so they are all types of being mindful.

There are many myths about mindfulness. Here are some reminders about what it is, and what it isn't:

Mindfulness is...	Mindfulness is not...
✓ Noticing your thoughts, feelings and body sensations.	✗ Making your mind go blank or getting rid of difficult thoughts.
✓ A simple technique that increases awareness of your body, mind and what's around you.	✗ A mysterious technique that takes years to learn.
✓ Helping you to improve your ability to focus and to switch your attention.	✗ Something that numbs your brain, gets rid of bad feelings or sends you to sleep.
✓ Learning to react to thoughts and difficult feelings in a different way.	✗ Achieved only by meditating for hours in silence.
✓ Helping you make positive choices about how to cope and enjoy life.	✗ Learning to never have negative thoughts again.

Try This 5 Minutes

Pay attention to daily activities

Doing an everyday activity, such as taking a shower or brushing your teeth, with a little more focus and awareness can help you appreciate these experiences, making them less boring and mundane, and bringing a small sense of positivity or enjoyment into your day. Why not try one of the following.

→ Notice the warmth and the refreshing flow of water as you take a shower and breathe in the smell of your favourite shower gel.

→ When you open the front door to collect a letter or parcel from someone, or when someone makes a meal or a drink for you, take a few seconds to make eye contact, smile and say thanks.

→ Focus on the refreshing feeling of cleaning your mouth whilst you brush your teeth.

→ Really listen to the person that you are talking to, giving them the benefit of your full attention.

→ Focus on feeling your body moving as you do any activity or exercise.

You could also pay extra attention to an activity that absorbs you, like painting, drawing, singing, playing a sport or even doing a chore. You might find this brings you 'into the zone' – not thinking about anything else and just paying attention to the one thing that you are doing at the time.

You might find this tricky at first but with only a few minutes of regular practice, it's possible to build your skills in focus and attention.

Which daily activities can you plan to pay more attention to? How will you remember to do this?

....

....

....

....

....

....

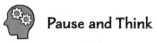 Pause and Think  5 Minutes

Autopilot versus being 'in the zone'

Can you think of a time that you were on autopilot, when your mind was so caught up that you didn't notice something else? What were you doing? What happened? What are the problems or advantages of being on autopilot?

How about being in the zone – can you think of any times that you were really engaged in something that you were doing? What was it about this activity that helped you stay focused? How did it feel to be in the zone?

 Try This  5 Minutes

Mindful drinking

Prepare by getting yourself a drink – it can be anything, even a glass of water.

You are going to slow down as if you are in a slow-motion video, and take a sip of your drink, using all your five senses: touch, sight, taste, hearing and smell.

Reach out slowly and pick up the glass or cup. Notice the feel of the glass, its weight, temperature and texture, as you pick it up.

Slowly lift it towards your mouth. Pause to smell your drink before trying it. Then take a small sip and hold it in your mouth. Notice the sensations, taste and temperature of the liquid on your tongue and in the rest of your mouth.

Notice the urge to swallow and hold it for a few seconds before you allow yourself to swallow and feel the sensations as it trickles down your throat.

Try again and see if you can notice something different about the experience this time. Imagine that you had never tried the drink before. How might you describe it to someone else?

Nihal was finding it difficult to focus at school and found his mind wandered off and he thought about what he was going to do later. He found himself thinking about the football scores… about lunchtime… everything except his lesson!

He found it difficult to absorb information because he was not listening and watching the teacher – and this was starting to worry him.

Nihal was sceptical when he heard about mindfulness. He thought it would be boring and he wouldn't be good at it but decided it was worth a try. He decided he would not worry about doing it well or trying too hard – he would just 'give it a go'.

He started by practising the everyday task of paying attention fully, using his five senses, whilst taking a shower. He noticed the sensations of the water, the smell of the shower gel and the sounds of the water spray for three minutes every morning.

At first, Nihal's mind wandered and he did not think it was helping. He thought he might not be doing it properly, but he kept going for four weeks.

Gradually, he became better able to notice when his mind was wandering and was able to bring it back to the sensations of the shower.

In class, he used this practice to 'ground' himself and bring his attention back to the lesson and what the teacher was saying, using his senses:

- **Sight**: He paused and looked for three different coloured objects in the room.

- **Touch**: He wriggled his toes and noticed the feel of his feet on the ground, and gently rubbed his fingers together.

- **Hearing**: He noticed two different sounds in the room and then he tuned in further to the teacher's voice.

Nihal found that the lesson was more interesting once he paid attention more and he was less worried about not passing his exam.

Pause and Think **5 Minutes**

Using your five senses

Using your five senses can be a great way to help you step out of autopilot and be more aware of what you are doing using sight, hearing, touch, taste and smell. We have already used most of these senses in the exercises that you have tried in this chapter so far.

What types of places or environments help you to use each of these senses to appreciate or pay attention to where you are or what you are doing more easily?

- → Do you notice or see things and get a sense of enjoyment outdoors? In woodland? By the sea? On a playing field? Looking down from a hilltop? Picture this in your mind.

- → Do you notice smells when you are in a freshly cut field? Shopping in a perfume shop? When you are cooking your favourite dish?

→ Do you notice sounds and different instruments when you are listening to music through your headphones? When you wake up early and hear birdsong? When the wind passes through the trees in a woodland? When there is chattering in the canteen?

→ Do you appreciate touch when you sink into the sofa? When a friend gives you a hug? When you wear something soft?

→ When do you appreciate taste most? When you are eating something rich and spicy? When you are having your first drink of the day?

Pause and Think   2 Minutes

Calm and soothing place

Close your eyes or lower your gaze and picture a calm or soothing place. Visualise this place for a few moments and describe it to yourself using your five senses.

→ What can you see? What colours, shapes, patterns shadows or changing light can you notice?

→ What sounds can you hear?

→ What can you feel or touch with your hands, feet, face and the rest of your body?

→ What can you taste or smell?

Now answer the following questions.

→ What things help you to be in the moment – fully concentrating on what you are doing?

→ What gets in the way of you being fully present? E.g. unhelpful thoughts, memories or pictures in your mind, emotions or body sensations?

Try This   5 Minutes

Mindful walking

Take a walk outside or around your room. As you walk, pay attention to your five senses. Take time to observe your surroundings, as if this is the first time you have walked in this place and you are planning to describe it to someone else. When you find yourself getting distracted, come back to paying attention to your walk.

→ What can you see around you? Look at where you are stepping. Can you avoid the cracks (or step on them)? What colours or shapes are there? Can you notice something you haven't seen before?

→ What can you hear? What sounds are you aware of?

→ Can you taste or smell anything?

→ What can you feel or touch? Pay attention to the sensation of your feet in contact with the ground. Try making each step extremely slow and deliberate and pay attention to the many tiny sensations in your feet and legs.

Mindful touch

Take any object in your hands, close your eyes and explore it with your hands and fingers. Notice the shape, texture and temperature of the object. You could also try gathering various fabrics such as silk, cotton, wool and velvet and notice whether they feel different or similar.

Repeat this activity using a different collection of objects, such as a stress ball, a stone, sandpaper, a crystal, plastic or a rubber.

Mindful photography

Choose somewhere quiet, either outside or inside, that you can walk and take photographs for up to 10 minutes without being disturbed.

Take a phone or camera with you. Look around and notice what you can see around you: What colours are there? What shapes? What patterns of light and shade?

Take photos of anything that your eye rests upon, anything that draws your attention. It might be a flower, a leaf, a shadow or an interesting shade of blue.

Your mind will wander during this exercise, and this is completely normal. As soon as you notice that your mind has drifted to another train of thought, just bring it back to the activity of looking and taking photos.

 **Try This** 🕐 **5 Minutes**

Mindful listening

Put on some music or listen to the sounds of nature or the natural sounds around you, such as the sound of traffic outside your window.

Close your eyes and tune in to your chosen sound(s). What is the loudest sound you can hear? What is the quietest sound?

If you are listening to music, follow the lyrics and notice the different instruments or how the singer's voice changes through the music. You might try noticing how often you hear a particular sound or lyric. If you have heard the song before, can you notice anything new about it?

Stay with the sound and come back to it when your mind throws up a distraction and you start thinking about something else.

Being open and making sense of your reactions

An important step in using being Open and Observing to help you cope with difficult experiences is to give a name or a label to each different part of your experience. This can help you to understand and recognise your own reactions to a particular situation.

Your reactions may involve pleasant experiences, such as feeling excitement as a warm tingling sensation that rises from the belly to the cheeks when you are looking forward to going somewhere. There may also be unpleasant body sensations, such as a sinking feeling in the stomach when you are disappointed by losing a rugby match or not getting a new job.

Our personal reactions are often complicated and can arise really quickly, so it's helpful to try to break these down and make sense of what's happening. Cognitive behavioural therapy (CBT) is known to help young people with emotional problems such as low mood and anxiety (NICE 2014; NICE 2019). It is based on the theory that there are links between how we think, feel (physically and emotionally) and behave. Breaking things down in this way can help you see things more clearly. You can use a simple CBT framework to explore your reactions to any event or situation, by looking at five different areas.

→ What you think.

→ How you feel – your emotions.

→ What's happening in your body – any physical sensations or reactions.

→ Your actions – what you do and don't do.

→ The situation and any triggers – what's happening around you?

Sometimes, it's hard to decide what is a thought, body sensation or a feeling. We will come back to this throughout the book, but here are some brief explanations.

→ **Thoughts**: Words, stories, ideas or images that we tell ourselves. They arise inside our mind and help us to make sense of what's happening around us.

→ **Emotions**: These are our inner feelings, such as anger, fear, joy and guilt.

→ **Physical sensations**: This involves noticing what you are feeling in your body. There are many reasons you might experience physical sensations, such as because you are touching something or because of illness or injury. Physical reactions often also arise when you experience an emotion.

→ **Behaviour**: This is what you do – what actions you choose to take. And remember, behaviour is the area that you have most control over. You might be able to notice the urge to carry out a behaviour before you do it – and you can then decide if it's helpful or not. It is far easier to control your behaviour than your thoughts or feelings.

→ **The situation, background or environment**: Where you are, who you are with, what your life experience has been so far, what you are paying attention to: all these external factors will influence how you feel and react at any given moment.

 **Try This**   **5 Minutes**

Using the CBT framework

Take a look at the following list. Underline any thoughts, feelings, body sensations and urges that you recognise. Draw lines to make links or match thoughts, body sensations and urges. Add any important ones of your own to the list.

Feelings	Thoughts	Body sensations	Actions and urges
Joyful	I am important	Fluttering	To dance
Happy	I can do this	Buzzing	To do exercise
Excited	I am interesting	Smiling	To chat to someone
Cheerful	This is fun	Lightness	To try something new
Proud	I am respected	Energetic	To keep going
Determined	I can cope with this		To play a game
Powerful	The future looks		
Hopeful	exciting		
Peaceful	I am cared about	Slow	To chill out
Calm	I am fulfilled	Relaxed	To listen to music
Relaxed	This is important to	Soft	To hug someone
Content	me	Warmth	
At ease	I am safe		
Satisfied			
Angry	This is stupid	Stiff	To punch a wall
Irritable	It's not fair	Headache	To yell at someone
Furious	This is wrong	Neck pain	To break something
Frustrated	They are uncaring	Clenched fists	To argue
Hostile	I feel rejected	Head/body rush	
Fed up		Hot (head, face, neck)	
		Tingling/prickles	
Scared	I feel threatened	Tense, fidgety	To pace around
Anxious	I can't cope	Tight chest	To hide
Insecure	I'm out of control	Butterflies	To ask for reassurance
Worried	This is dangerous	Shaking	To check my phone
Fearful	I'm unsafe	Racing heart	To run away
Panicky		Sweaty palms	
		Feeling sick	
		Frozen/unable to move	
Embarrassed	I'm not important	Heartache	To lash out
Ashamed	I look foolish	Numb	To eat something
Jealous	They are mean	Burning	unhealthy
Lonely	I'm being left out	Flushed cheeks	To get my own back
Sad	I can't be bothered	Aching	To lie down and rest
Guilty	I am useless	Heavy body/chest	To give up and stop
Lethargic	I am stupid	Sinking	trying
Bored	What's the point?	Tiredness	To avoid everyone
Miserable		Brain-fog	
		Headache	

Other feelings:	Other thoughts:	Other body sensations:	Other urges:

 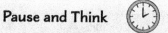 **Pause and Think** 🕐 **10 Minutes**

Think about a time that you recently experienced a difficult feeling or emotion; nothing too overwhelming – perhaps a time that you felt slightly stressed, nervous, irritable or fed up.

→ Use the chart above to help answer the following questions and complete the blank chart below.

→ What was the situation? What else was affecting you?

→ What were you thinking?

→ How did you feel? What emotions came up?

→ What was happening in your body?

→ What did you do?

....

....

....

....

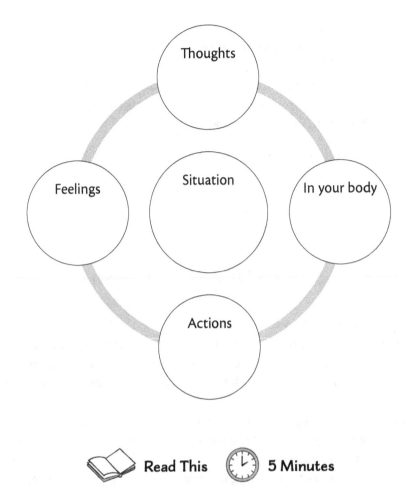

Read This — 5 Minutes

Robbie is studying at sixth form college. He struggles with maths and physics but enjoys human biology and sports and has ambitions to study sports science. He is competitive and likes to do well, particularly in rugby, and plays for a team at the weekend. This Saturday they had a heavy defeat, which made him feel low in mood. He notices that he gets a sensation like there is a hole in his stomach when he feels low, and he eats more junk food to compensate.

Robbie is also stressed, as there are exams coming up that he needs to pass. When he is feeling anxious, he notices tingling in his muscles and his thoughts race more, giving him tension in his neck and head — he describes it as 'feeling wired'.

Bruno, who is in the same maths class and was on the opposing team, taunts Robbie as he comes into the classroom on Monday. Robbie has the urge to lash out and punch Bruno, but because he is tuned in to the tingling sensation he gets at the back of his neck when he is really angry, he is able to ignore the comments, let a slow breath out and just get his books out, before replying with, 'Don't get smug — we beat you last year and we'll see how the next match works out, Bruno...'

Pause and Think  **5 Minutes**

Can you pick out Robbie's body sensations, emotions and thoughts? How did being Open and noticing sensations, thoughts and emotions help with Robbie's reaction to the incident?

....

....

....

Read This **10 Minutes**

Making space and stepping back

Hopefully, you will already have found that this is a practical workbook with information, exercises and tools to help you get the best out of life. We are now going to think about doing something completely different: stop trying to solve or get rid of your difficulties!

This sounds like the opposite of what your instincts might tell you to do. The problem is that fighting to get rid of difficult thoughts and feelings takes a lot of effort and brain energy but is often unsuccessful.

Instead, you could try being **willing** to experience whatever comes up: make some space inside to experience difficulties and discomfort, which might be a signal that you are about to do something important. You could stop struggling to get rid of problems you cannot solve and focus on living the life you choose, in spite of or alongside negative thoughts and feelings.

This involves focusing on the things that you can change and learning to accept some of the things that you cannot change. And this includes recognising that it's not possible to just get rid of difficult thoughts and feelings. You may need to take them along on the journey.

We can use being Open and Observing to help with this. You could try stepping back and noticing the unwanted body sensation, thought, emotion, urge, brain-fog, overwhelm, or whatever the discomfort is. You can recognise that the uncomfortable thought or feeling is present, and then give it a bit of room to pass in its own time, without fighting to feel differently, shut it out or avoid it, which often only makes things worse.

What you **can** control is your behaviour (what you choose to do) and your attention (where you choose to focus your awareness).

You might be a little sceptical and wonder if this really works! And that's fine, we invite you to try this out for yourself. To experiment and discover what's best for **you**. It might sound like quite a challenge, so think about the skills you have learned so far that might help.

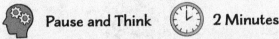

Pause and Think   2 Minutes

Getting caught up versus making space

Have you ever got so caught up in thoughts and feelings that you stopped being able to enjoy the present moment, do something important or be 'in the zone'? Have you ever:

→ completely missed what someone was saying because you were too focused on what you were going to say next

→ walked straight past a friend, as you were caught up in your own mind thinking about something bad that happened

→ been unable to enjoy your favourite meal because you had something on your mind

→ found that your performance was affected by doubts or worries that something might go wrong?

Notice and name what happened:

→ **Thoughts**: What went through your mind? What words or images came up?

→ **Feelings**: What emotions did you experience?

→ **In the body**: What physical sensations were you aware of?

→ **Behaviour and urges**: What urges did you experience? Did you act on these? What did you do? Was it helpful or unhelpful in this situation?

→ **Around you**: Who or what was important in your environment that affected you or the situation?

....

....

....

....

Listen to This   **3 Minutes**

TUNING IN

Read This   **3 Minutes**

Surfing with your Guide

Being able to cope with the difficult thoughts, feelings, urges and all the other discomfort that goes along with being human brings many benefits and a sense of freedom. And it helps if you continue Following your Guide, doing the things you know are important and becoming the person you want to be, despite any difficulties that pop up on the way.

You could think of this as surfing a wave and staying on your board, feeling the thrill of riding over it. Or going over a bump in the road and continuing to stay on track, even if you experience some problems or negative thoughts and feelings, such as anxiety, low mood or irritation.

Pause and Think   **5 Minutes**

Don't let distractions ruin the movie!

Imagine you are settled in the cinema, getting ready to watch a great movie. Suddenly, the person in front pulls out a huge bag of popcorn and starts crunching away noisily, distracting you from the film. You can't force the person to leave the cinema, and you don't want to go home and end up missing a film that you've been looking forward to for ages. You could spend all your time watching the person, shushing them and generally complaining about the noise they are making, but this just distracts you from the movie and spoils your enjoyment...

So, what's the alternative? Well, you could try just accepting that the person is there, which you cannot do much about, and that they are making a noise, which is annoying. But Following your Guide means that you don't want to allow this to ruin your movie experience completely.

So, you have acknowledged and made sense of the experience and labelled the feeling, and now you have another option. You can shift your attention back to the film and focus on that. You might use your five senses, enjoying the smell and taste of your own popcorn, taking a sip of your drink, listening to the music and the sounds of the movie or concentrating on the visual experience of watching a film – using the Open and Observing mindfulness skills we have been looking at in this chapter. You might find that this starts to cut down your awareness of the popcorn-munching person and that, before you know it, they have finished the box and are being quiet again. This is not always easy, especially if your emotions are high, but it usually gets easier with time and with practice.

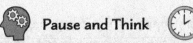 **Pause and Think** **5 Minutes**

Following your Guide when life is uncomfortable

Think of a time when you felt apprehensive about doing something and had difficult thoughts and feelings but did it anyway because it was really important to you. Maybe you spoke up for someone, completed a sports challenge, sat an exam, went into a new situation...

Describe your own example here:

Now answer these questions.

→ What uncomfortable thoughts and feelings did you overcome in order to do this?

→ What important values were you moving towards?

→ How does it feel, right now in this moment, when you think about this?

→ Was it worth it in the long run?

What we have covered in Chapter 3: Open and Observing

→ You learned some mindfulness skills that have benefits in improving focus and coping with difficult feelings and body sensations.

→ You practised some Open and Observing exercises to help you appreciate the here and now and to focus or shift attention when you notice your mind has drifted away from the present moment.

→ You discovered how to make sense of what we are experiencing at any moment, using a CBT framework to break it down into thoughts, feelings, body sensations, actions and what's around us in the external world.

→ You explored some ways of stepping back and observing difficult emotions rather than getting caught up, stuck or overwhelmed by them.

→ You reminded yourself to continue to Follow your Guide and to do what matters to you – even if that means some short-term discomfort.

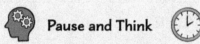 **Pause and Think**   **5 Minutes**

Make a note of anything that you found particularly helpful, interesting or surprising in this chapter:

....

....

....

What next?

Choose one small action for the coming week based on what you have read so far. Can you commit to practising some of the skills? Anything else?

Writing it down will help you remember. It will also help you to commit to doing something differently.

....

....

....

Chapter 4

WISE MIND

→ Have you ever missed out on something because a negative voice in your head said: 'You'll never do it – you'll fail and look stupid'?

→ Do you ever get stuck in negative loops in your mind that endlessly go over problems from the past or worry about scary possibilities in the future?

→ Does it seem like you are repeating the same patterns and allowing old habits to take control of your life, or are you making reasoned, thoughtful decisions?

→ Do you want to develop your Wise Mind? Read on...

 **Read This** **5 Minutes**

What is Wise Mind?

Your mind is made up of the thoughts, beliefs, stories and images that allow you to make sense of the world. These lie within your own personal inner world and are invisible to others, but what appears in your mind will be influenced by many things, including your personality, events in your life and the people around you, both past and present. All of this affects how you feel and react.

Wise Mind involves balancing logic and emotions: using your reasoning and evaluating skills, which are unique to us as human beings, coupled with your capacity to feel emotions and empathise with the feelings of others. Listening to your Wise Mind will enable you to make helpful choices about what action to take in any situation. It involves looking at the big picture and thinking flexibly – adapting your perspective to meet each new challenge.

It may take time and practice to develop Wise Mind skills and learn how to use it in your own life. Following your Wise Mind may also require courage as you make and follow through with Wise decisions that will help you thrive, and act with choice as you Follow your Guide, whilst remaining Open and Observing your own thoughts, feelings and urges to react in any situation.

In this chapter, we will:

→ notice any unhelpful thought patterns and emotions that may stop you from Following your Guide

→ spot the points at which you have a choice about what thoughts to listen to and what actions to take

→ learn to recognise negative thoughts without struggling to get rid of them using techniques such as labelling and creating a mental caricature of the thought

→ learn some skills for getting 'unhooked' from negative thoughts linked to strong emotions

→ discover how to make Wise choices about helpful actions when facing a challenging situation.

 **Watch This** **3 Minutes**

WISE MIND VIDEO

 Pause and Think **2 Minutes**

What is your reaction to the video? What's the most important thing you took away from watching it?

....

....

....

....

📖 **Read This** 🕐 **10 Minutes**

Noticing unhelpful thought patterns and reactions

In the first two chapters, we looked at ways to Follow your Guide and some of the things that can get in the way of taking positive steps and being Ready for Action.

We have all experienced times when negative thinking patterns, such as worrying about what might go wrong or having self-critical or defeatist thoughts, have pulled us away from what we care about and prevented us from living the full, rich and meaningful life we would wish for.

When you are feeling stressed or are in a highly charged emotional state, such as feeling angry, hurt, fearful or impatient, you may be prone to acting on impulse. Your emotions have hijacked your actions and you might make snap decisions that bypass your usual logic, reasoning or ability to think of others, and that you might not have made if you were feeling calmer and had more time to decide what to do.

This is where Wise Mind comes in. Rather than following the same old patterns or acting purely based on emotions or impulse, Wise Mind helps you get perspective, take a step back and walk the fine line that takes into account logic and reasoning **and** your own feelings about the situation. This helps you make choices and take actions that work for you – and others.

Freddie was the second eldest in a family of four. He loved his family and had a close relationship with his brother, Benjamin, who was in the year above him at school. They had always been good buddies. Benjamin loved maths and science and had won many prizes for his school studies. Academic achievement was an important value in Freddie's family and the boys' parents were very proud of these awards.

Freddie worked hard at school but he really preferred more practical subjects like design technology. During one of his design classes, Freddie produced a great piece of furniture, which was highly praised by his father and mother.

But instead of recognising the compliments he was given and following what he enjoyed and valued, Freddie started to feel disheartened, because he never did as well academically as his brother. His inner critic told him that he wasn't as good as his brother and that he would fail in life.

Freddie felt resentful towards Benjamin for his achievements and the praise he received at school. He started to notice a tightness in his chest and neck and began getting headaches. He became irritable and snappy at home and started to pick arguments and criticise and taunt his brother, so their relationship began to deteriorate.

Freddie became more and more stressed as exams loomed, staying up late revising to try to get better results than his brother. He was determined to beat him for once!

One morning, after he had not slept well at all, his brother asked him to pass the milk. He shouted, 'Get it yourself — I'm not your servant,' slammed down his bowl so it smashed and stormed out.

Freddie was exhausted, unhappy and was getting into trouble at home and at school.

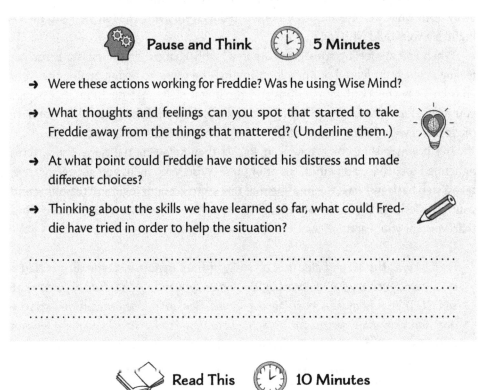

Pause and Think   **5 Minutes**

→ Were these actions working for Freddie? Was he using Wise Mind?

→ What thoughts and feelings can you spot that started to take Freddie away from the things that mattered? (Underline them.)

→ At what point could Freddie have noticed his distress and made different choices?

→ Thinking about the skills we have learned so far, what could Freddie have tried in order to help the situation?

....

....

....

Read This   **10 Minutes**

Unwanted Mind Visitors

Negative thoughts can be a bit like unwanted guests who turn up in your mind, causing disruption and spoiling your enjoyment of a situation. These thoughts usually come along with emotions such as fear, anger, self-doubt and low mood, and can be very loud and demanding. Unhelpful thoughts can often lead to unhelpful reactions such as...

→ deciding to give up and stop trying when you face a problem

→ pushing away or avoiding important people in your life

→ deciding not to take on a new challenge because you fear you might fail.

The following diagram shows some examples of some of the Unwanted Mind Visitors that might sometimes appear as negative thoughts, causing distress and getting in the way of achieving your goals.

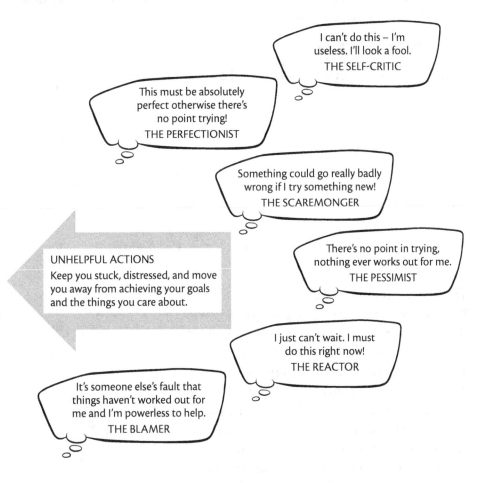

This is not a complete list – there are many more, but you can see how listening to these thoughts could lead to unhelpful behaviours or actions, which might lead you away from some of your important values.

 **Pause and Think** **10 Minutes**

Who are your most common unwelcome thought visitors?

➜ Think of a difficult challenge that you have been facing recently. What types of negative thoughts tend to pop up in your mind?

→ How does this make you feel?

→ How do the thoughts affect your behaviour or actions? What do you have the urge to do when you are thinking this way?

→ What might be the long-term effects of acting in this way?

→ Notice your choices: What other choices do you have for your actions?

. . . .

. . . .

. . . .

 **Read This** 🕐 **10 Minutes**

Thoughts are not facts

Thoughts are mental events that pop up in the mind. They come and go and can change with your mood. When you are feeling happy and upbeat, you are more likely to experience optimistic and positive thoughts about things going well. This is sometimes known as having 'rose-tinted' glasses. Similarly, when you are feeling fed up, irritable or anxious, you may be more likely to see the world in a gloomy light.

It's important to keep in mind that you are not your thoughts, and you don't have to believe every single thought that you experience.

Thoughts are temporary and can change. They represent just one opinion or viewpoint and may need to be updated when you learn new facts. It's possible to have both positive and negative thoughts about the same issue on different days. You can even deliberately choose to think something that's not true, such as, 'I have purple hair' (or whatever colour hair you don't have!).

However, these thinking patterns can shape your reality by affecting the actions that you choose to take. And whilst you cannot choose or control the thoughts that pop into your mind, you can choose and control the behaviour that you take in response to the thoughts.

Let go of the struggle

People often say that they wish they could just rid themselves of their negative thoughts. But even though you might recognise that some of your thinking patterns are unhelpful, it can be hard to change these. In fact, it's not possible to just stop yourself from having thoughts that you don't want! And often, the harder you try to get rid of negative thoughts and feelings, the stronger they can grow.

Pushing away negative thoughts takes a lot of effort, is tiring, can leave you feeling frustrated and takes your attention away from doing other things that matter to you.

An alternative option is to let the thought be there for a while – acknowledge it, allow it and accept it. This doesn't mean that you have to agree with the thought or do what it says if this behaviour is unhelpful for you. But letting go of the struggle to stop thinking negatively gives the thought less power and intensity and may make it easier to make Wise choices, even if the thought is still present.

The key is to be aware of your thoughts and feelings and catch them at the point at which you can make a choice about what action to take in response to them – to 'freeze frame' and create a tiny pause, just long enough for Wise Mind to step in and influence your actions and the outcome.

So, how do you allow a thought to be present without struggling? There are many ways to do this. Why not try out some of the following techniques and see if you find any of them helpful.

Scroll past like on social media

When you are experiencing strong emotions, it's easy to get caught up in your mind and start to see your thoughts as being completely true rather than being just one perspective or point of view. But it's important to remember that your thoughts are not facts – even the ones that say they are!

Try viewing your thoughts as social media posts. Saying, 'I'm feeling sad because my mind just "posted" a negative comment about how my friend feels about me,' is very different to really believing the thought that, 'She doesn't like me.'

If you are scrolling through social media and you come to a post that's negative or unhelpful, you have a choice. You might decide to stop and read it and perhaps start disagreeing and arguing with whoever made the post. But this often gives more time and attention to the negative post than you would really like and prevents you from doing other things.

Another option is to simply continue scrolling. Ignore the negative post and move on to do something more interesting and important. Similarly, you can choose to scroll past negative thoughts.

 **Do This** **3 Minutes**

SCROLL PAST YOUR THOUGHTS

Next time a negative or unhelpful thought pops up into your mind, try scrolling past as if it were a social media post.

Say to yourself, 'My mind is posting thoughts again,' or think of it like an annoying pop-up advert.

Remember, you don't have to click on the advert, spend time engaging with the negative post or react to the thought.

Can you simply move on and do something else that's more important?

Label your thoughts

Giving your thoughts a label by saying, 'This is a thought,' can create some perspective and space when you are having negative thoughts. As with most things, you might need to practise these skills, so that they become a healthy mind habit that's ready and available when you need it. There are lots of ways to practise labelling your thoughts, such as the following.

→ **Talk out loud and describe what's happening in your mind**: Try saying to yourself, 'I'm having the thought that I'm going to mess up,' rather than, 'I'm going to mess up.'

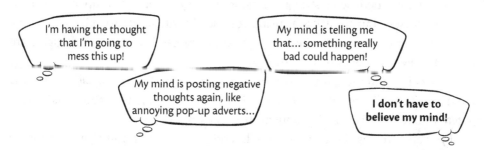

→ **Post-it note thoughts**: Write the thought on a post-it note or imagine yourself doing this.

→ **Bad weather thoughts**: View negative thoughts and feelings like a temporary change in the weather. Clouds may come and it may rain for a while, but sooner or later, the clouds will pass and the sun will come out again, so it's not necessary to take the thoughts too seriously.

Pause and Think   **10 Minutes**

Hooks and urges

It can be one thing to recognise that negative thoughts are extreme and unrealistic, but many thoughts are very powerful and just **feel very true**, especially when accompanied by powerful emotions.

Think about someone who is completely overtaken with rage and anger.

What kinds of thoughts do they have? How well is someone who is in a furious rage able to look at the big picture and see another person's perspective?

Mostly, experiencing any strong emotion makes us less likely to think rationally, clearly and accurately. We are more likely to think in extreme and unrealistic ways that are one-sided and don't take other people's points of view into account.

But how much does the angry person believe that they are right?

Someone who has very strong emotions such as anger is less likely to see the world accurately and clearly, but they are more likely to believe that they are right.

This is because strong emotions makes the thought **feel** true and convincing, even when it may be completely exaggerated and unrealistic. And these strong emotions can create a 'hook' that pulls us rapidly towards unhelpful behaviour. Other 'hooks' include wanting to avoid discomfort such as feeling anxious or embarrassed, or slipping into unhelpful habits or short-term gains such as comfort eating and delay tactics.

Mind Train exercise

1. Bring a slightly distressing or annoying experience to mind. Don't choose anything too upsetting or powerful, just something that brings up a mild negative feeling.

2. Ask yourself: What thoughts and feelings am I having?

3. Instead of getting 'hooked' by the thoughts and feelings, imagine that you are attaching each one to the carriage of a long, rumbling train.

4. Watch the train pass by without getting on.

5. Remind yourself that the thoughts and feelings may be uncomfortable for a while but will pass if you pause and wait.

6. You **don't** have to jump on board! You don't have to react immediately.

7. Stay on the platform and choose which train to get on – pick one that is going to a destination you want to visit!

8. Allow any difficult thoughts and feelings to pass by on the Mind Train.

Here are some more methods of 'unhooking' from unhelpful thoughts.

Use a silly voice

Try using a voice changer app that repeats back what you say in a funny voice. Hearing your negative thoughts said in a growl, spoken by Darth Vader or turned into a rap might help you to recognise that what you are saying is a thought, assumption or belief rather than a definite fact. This can be fun, and using humour can be a great tool for defusing negative thoughts.

If you don't have your phone, you could just go somewhere that you won't be disturbed and try saying the thoughts out loud in a silly voice. How does it feel to sing the thoughts or quack them like Donald Duck?

Create an image or caricature

Think back to the Unwanted Mind Visitors that we talked about: the Scaremonger, the Pessimist, the Self-Critic... Which of those characters most often pops up and spoils the moment? Creating an image or caricature to go with the thought can help you to see it as separate from yourself and gives it less power.

Would you really choose to listen to someone giving you advice or telling you what to do if they were known to be a large crow who only ever caws bad news loudly and repeatedly and struts about bullying and blaming other people for everything?

CREATE AN IMAGE TO GO WITH THE NEGATIVE VOICE

Can you create a mental picture of what it might look like? Is it a grumbling gremlin? A squawking, repetitive parrot? A gloomy ghost or an owl?

If you can make the image memorable and funny in some way, it will be much more effective. You could even draw a picture of it!

What kind of voice would this character have?

Now try to imagine them saying one of your thoughts in their whiny, grumbling voice.

Let them say what they need to – there's no need to argue or disagree. Imagine politely moving your mind character to a back room, so you don't have to pay so much attention to it. You can even thank them for their comments before deciding what to do next.

You don't have to follow their advice or believe their negative view of the world if it's unhelpful.

Calming powerful emotions

Sometimes, powerful emotions such as anger or hurt can lead us to react in ways we regret afterwards. The surge of emotions activates our 'fight or flight' response and we act on impulse, often bypassing our Wise Mind.

What might help is to keep up your regular practice with Open and Observe skills and to have some quick 'first aid' tools to take the heat out of strong emotions.

Remember, it helps to practise these skills when you **don't** need them so that they kick into action when you **do** need them. You are cultivating Wise Mind. They become part of you.

 **Try This**  **1 Minute**

STOP:

1. **S**pot a struggle and Stop what you are doing – 'freeze frame'.

2. **T**ake a breath from deep in your belly and exhale as slowly as possible.

3. **O**bserve your thoughts and feelings – notice and name what's happening.

4. **P**roceed: Allow Wise Mind to help you choose what to do next and proceed with Wise actions.

Listen to This **5 Minutes**

PRESS PAUSE AND REPLAY

 Read This   🕐 10 Minutes

Wise choices

Think back to Chapter 2 when we talked about being Ready for Action and choosing life-fulfilling and life-enhancing actions that take you towards things that you care about rather than moving in the opposite direction by engaging with thoughts, feelings and life-draining activities that keep you stuck.

It's sometimes useful to think about Wise Mind as a bridge, helping you over a turbulent river (unhelpful thoughts, feelings, urges and memories) and allowing you to make Wise choices and take Wise actions to cross over towards what you care about. The bridge is the point at which there is **choice**.

Wise Mind is like a supportive coach, encouraging you to keep going when things are tough, coaxing you across the bridge and sometimes suggesting new ways of doing things to make improvements (ensuring that you learn and develop) and suggesting you try things more than once if they do not work first time. Remember that you always have choices about what action to take, no matter what the negative voice is saying.

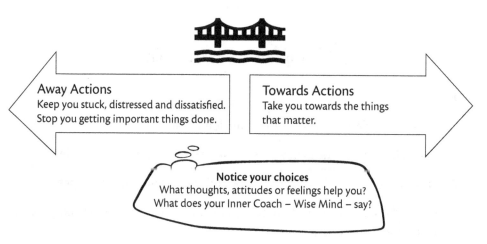

Away Actions
Keep you stuck, distressed and dissatisfied. Stop you getting important things done.

Towards Actions
Take you towards the things that matter.

Notice your choices
What thoughts, attitudes or feelings help you?
What does your Inner Coach – Wise Mind – say?

What makes a Wise Mind?

Notice your choices

The first step in developing your own Wise Mind is to remember that you always have choices in your actions. You may not be able to choose a specific desired outcome, but you can choose what action to take when faced with any problem: whether to walk away, talk to someone, take a sip of your drink, read a book or study for a test. We have many choices and make many of these without even realising that we are doing so.

So, which action should you choose at any particular time? Wise Mind can help here too.

Is this helpful for me?

One of the key questions that Wise Mind asks about every action that you choose to take is, 'How helpful is this action for me?'.

Your Guide can help with this. For each action, ask yourself: Is this action moving me **towards** or **away** from my values and the things that matter to me?

This can change and may depend on the context. For example, watching a TV programme could be helpful and move you towards a value of relaxation and fun. But if you watch TV for hours on end and use it to avoid doing something else that's important, such as revising for an exam, it's moving you away from your value of achievement.

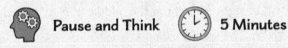 **Pause and Think**   **5 Minutes**

Bring a challenging situation to mind or choose something that you've been putting off or avoiding for some reason. What negative thoughts pop up for you? Choose one and then ask yourself these questions.

→ Is this thought (mindset, urge, action) helping me?

→ Which value is important to me? Where is my Guide pointing?

→ If I let this thought guide my behaviour, in which direction will it take me?

→ Does it help me to be the person I want to be and do the things I want to do?

→ If not, where is it taking me?

....
....
....
....

Take a helicopter view

Wise Mind takes a big-picture view of any situation, looking for different perspectives without getting too caught up in small details. This can help you learn to think more flexibly and adapt your reactions to match each new challenge that you face.

 **Pause and Think** **5 Minutes**

Think of a recent argument or disagreement you have had with a sibling or school friend where you got caught up in some unhelpful reactions that might have been helped by taking a different viewpoint. If you are struggling to think of something, look back at the example at the beginning of the chapter with Freddie and his brother Benjamin.

Imagine yourself rising above the situation in a helicopter to get a view from above rather than being stuck right in the middle of it. What would the view look like from up there?

Now answer the following questions.

→ **Your view**: How do you see things? What does this situation mean to you?

→ **Others**: How might things look to others involved?

→ **Outsider**: How would this seem to someone who is not emotionally involved with the situation?

→ **Shifting time**: How might this seem six months from now? How about in a year? What about in five years? Does this change your perspective?

→ **Wise Mind**: What would be the best thing (for you and others) in this situation?

....

....

....

....

....

Putting it all together

So, now you have learned some new skills, the next part is to put this all together using your Guide and being Ready for Action – taking steps in the direction of what you care about in order to lead a life that has meaning and purpose. And when you come to a choice point, being able to 'freeze frame' for just long enough to use Open and Observe skills to listen to your Wise Mind and make helpful choices that take you towards your values.

Sometimes, there may be a cost to Following your Guide. The cost is being willing to experience discomfort – being Open to distressing thoughts and feelings in the pursuit of what is important. You may need to remind yourself that it's worth it! Try to keep your values in mind – this can help motivate you to keep going when things are difficult.

The Golden Ticket

Your values – who and what is important to you – are like a Golden Ticket. They are something you aspire to and desire, but the price of the ticket may be that you need to experience some short-term discomfort to bring your values to life and achieve your goals. You can then decide if the Golden Ticket is worth the price.

 Read This 5 Minutes

THE PRICE ON THE TICKET

Hannah's best friend Joti had moved to a new house in the next town, but they kept in contact regularly and visited each other during holidays.

Hannah had recently become anxious about travelling, particularly on crowded trains. She did not like the feeling of being enclosed or being hot and sweaty. Once she had experienced an increased heart rate and difficulty breathing whilst on a train and she thought she was going to faint. She got off the train at the next station, called Joti to make an excuse and went back home. She hadn't been to see her friend since this experience. Joti kept asking if she had done anything to upset Hannah, who felt embarrassed to explain how she felt. She also feared losing contact with her best friend.

Hannah thought about what would happen if she continued to make excuses and avoid going on the train. What if she continued listening to the Scaremonger character that popped into her mind, telling her that the train might break down and she could be stranded on a crowded train for hours... even though this had never happened? What would be the cost in terms of her friendship?

Hannah decided that she wasn't willing to pay the price of listening to her fears. She pictured the Scaremonger as a wicked witch with a cackling voice and reminded herself that witches exist only in fables. She tried to see the situation from Joti's viewpoint and thought about how their friendship would slip away if she continued to avoid trains for the next five years. She used her Wise Mind to help her make a choice about what to do next.

She decided that the price she had to pay to keep in touch with her friend was to be willing to experience some discomfort. She decided to try to use some Open and Observing skills to help her to get back on the train. She used the Mind Train exercise (page 77) to prepare herself and during the journey when she started to feel uncomfortable. She also distracted herself by looking out of the window and playing games on her phone. She arrived at Joti's house and felt really pleased she had made the effort. They had a great time together as always – the ticket was well worth the price.

A few weeks later, she still felt a little nervous about travelling by train but was starting to build her confidence, and each time she tried it became a little easier. Best of all, Hannah felt proud of herself for starting to do the things that were most important to her.

What we have covered in Chapter 4: Wise Mind

→ Wise Mind is about balancing logic and emotions, looking at the big picture and thinking flexibly, enabling you to make helpful choices about what action to take in any situation.

→ Thoughts are not always facts, but they can strongly influence how you feel, how you react and what you choose to do. However, you don't have to believe your mind if what it is telling you is unhelpful or taking you away from your values.

→ You can view unhelpful thought patterns as Unwanted Mind Visitors, such as the Pessimist or the Scaremonger. You can learn to spot when they show up, and, by creating an image and even a silly voice, you can step back and let go of the struggle so they become less powerful and overwhelming.

→ There are many ways to 'unhook' from difficult thoughts and urges, such as scrolling past like social media, using the STOP technique, putting difficult thoughts on the Mind Train and labelling uncomfortable thoughts and feelings.

→ Wise Mind helps you 'surf' discomfort and make Wise choices, helping you to keep Following your Guide as you choose how to respond to life's challenges.

We have now covered the GROW model in full and the rest of book will help you to apply this to a wide range of different situations, emotions and experiences.

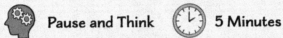 **Pause and Think** **5 Minutes**

→ What are the most important messages for you from this chapter?

→ What have you learned or understood after reading it and trying the exercises?

....
....
....
....

What next?

→ What are you going to do differently now?

→ What can you keep practising on a regular basis?

→ What is your first step?

....
....
....
....

Chapter 5

UNDERSTANDING YOUR BRAIN AND YOUR EMOTIONS

→ Are you super-sensitive and find that a wave of strong emotion often hits you out of nowhere?

→ Is it hard to control your reactions, and do you find yourself saying or doing things on impulse?

→ Do you want to understand and cope with your feelings and reactions better?

→ Understand your brain and learn how to apply your 10 Minute GROW skills! Read on...

 **Read This** 🕐 **5 Minutes**

Understanding emotions

In this chapter, we will give an overview of some key facts about your brain and the different emotional systems, which can affect how you think and what you do, and how these may link to the GROW skills we have learned in Part 1 of this book.

We will look at the following areas.

→ **The developing brain**: We will learn how changes in brain structure and chemistry between the ages of 10 and 24 affect the nervous system and emotions, your ability to focus and learn, and your patterns of behaviour.

→ **The three emotion systems**: We will discover ways of finding balance between the Threat, Drive and Achieve, and Calm, Care and Connect systems, helping you maximise your physical and emotional wellbeing by learning to cope with scary or threatening situations, achieve the things that matter to you and find ways to calm, settle, connect and recharge your energy.

→ **The importance of kindness:** We will learn how showing kindness and empathy towards ourselves and others can help us cope with difficult emotions and to understand and respect the feelings and needs of others.

Read This **5 Minutes**

The developing brain

Your brain is amazing – it can fit in the palm of your hand, and there are ten times more cells in the brain than there are people on the planet!

Your brain controls all the basic functions in your body, enabling you to think, talk, feel, see, hear, breathe, walk and much more. Some of the more specialised tasks that the brain controls include intelligence, creativity, emotion and memory.

The brain is thought to be fully 'mature' at around the age of 25, but different parts of the brain develop at different times. And even after this age, your brain can continue to change in response to experiences throughout your life.

The key message is that your brain is in a state of development! It has lots of **plasticity**, which means it can change, adapt and 'rewire' in response to the environment. Carrying out challenging mental activities, doing exercise and being creative can all help the brain to GROW and learn.

Learning about your brain can help you find ways to manage your emotions, and to think and behave differently. There are also changes in the brain that can make things more challenging for young people, and it can be helpful to understand what these are and look for the best ways to live your life using your incredible brain.

Read This **10 Minutes**

How your brain develops

One of the most rapid stages of brain development during our lifetime happens between the ages of around 11 and 24. The brain does not grow by getting much larger, but it develops stronger and faster nerve connections. During this period, lots of new connections are made between the nerve cells (neurons) in the brain. This means that there is a huge potential for new learning and is why it's easier for young people to learn new knowledge and skills than adults.

The connections between neurons in the brain grow stronger whenever you learn something new. And the more times you do something and repeat it, the more the connections will strengthen and increase. Over time, as you regularly practise a new skill, your brain builds a pathway of neurons that connect together, and your skills grow into habits.

Any connections between neurons that are not used regularly die away while the ones that are used regularly remain and get stronger. This is known as 'pruning' and it allows your brain to adapt to the unique circumstances of your life. It also means that if you don't continue to practise skills, you can lose them.

During later adolescence, the connections between brain cells that are used most often are made extra fast and efficient in a process called 'myelination'. Myelin is an insulating layer around connections of brain cells. This insulation allows connections to be made more quickly and efficiently. This means you can become expert at certain skills or activities.

Brain pathways

The networks of connections between neurons in your brain are like paths through a forest. As you walk along a particular route more often, the path becomes more worn and obvious, the grass and undergrowth are flattened and it becomes easier to travel down it next time.

In the same way, whenever you regularly focus on something with your thoughts, feelings and behaviours, you strengthen these brain pathways and create a well-worn pathway or mental habit.

And if you don't walk that way often, the path will become overgrown and more difficult to find or follow.

This helps build skills such as playing sports, learning a musical instrument or speaking another language. It is also true for emotional habits and reactions, such as the types of thoughts, feelings and actions that you tend to fall back on in stressful situations.

You can actively train your brain to develop pathways by practising important skills. These could be practical skills as well as skills in managing emotions. So, you can practise your GROW skills and, over time, these will become well-worn brain pathways that you can easily fall back on when you need them.

 **Read This** 🕐 **10 Minutes**

Different parts of the brain

The brain is divided into two halves: the right and left hemispheres. These are joined by a bridge called the corpus callosum, which transmits messages from one side to the other. The two sides of the brain have different responsibilities. In general, the left hemisphere controls speech, comprehension, arithmetic and writing. The right hemisphere controls creativity, spatial ability, artistic skills and musical skills.

A quick and simple way to understand the brain, which is helpful for understanding your emotions and behaviour, is to think about it in three parts.

→ **Higher brain**: This is the most sophisticated part of your brain, where you carry out thinking, planning and reasoning.

→ **Limbic system**: This is responsible for emotions and memory.

→ **Brainstem**: This is the part of the brain that is responsible for basic body functions and survival. It links to the spinal cord and the nervous system throughout the body. This is one of the oldest parts of the brain from an evolutionary point of view and is also known as the 'reptilian brain'.

Areas of the brain

 **Try This** 🕐 **1 Minute**

MAKE YOUR BRAIN WITH ONE HAND!

You can imagine how your brain is organised by looking at your hand!

1. Make a fist with your thumb curled inside.

2. Your wrist is like the brainstem, which connects the brain to the spinal cord and the rest of the body.

3. Your thumb is like the limbic system, in the centre of the brain.

4. Your fingers are like the higher brain, which is the outer part of the brain.

What does each part of the brain do?

Each part of the brain is responsible for a different set of jobs and responsibilities. We have summarised these in the chart below.

Part of brain	Which areas are involved?	What does it do?
The higher brain	Cerebral cortex (grey matter) including the prefrontal cortex (PFC).	The wrinkly outer layer of the brain contains the higher brain. This is the rational part of your brain, which has a vital role in thinking, planning, problem-solving, self-control and awareness. The higher brain does not finish developing until around 25 years of age, when it starts to tame impulses and helps with making decisions. Before this age, young people may be more prone to impulsive or risky actions and find it harder to focus or judge outcomes.
The limbic system	This is made up of several areas, including the hippocampus, thalamus and amygdala.	The limbic system is buried deep within the brain, and controls emotions, reward-seeking actions and memory. It will help you decide whether to move towards something that you want or move away from something that seems dangerous. The limbic brain may 'take charge' when emotions are high, especially in young people where the higher brain has not fully developed. This leads to rollercoaster emotions and being more likely to take high risks and seek instant rewards.
Brainstem (reptilian brain)	The brainstem links to the spinal cord and the nervous system in the body.	The brainstem controls most of the body's essential functions, such as blood pressure, temperature, sleep cycles and digestion. It is also involved in the automatic survival system, the fight or flight (threat) response, by controlling the heartbeat, breathing and sweating.

Emotions and decision-making

As we have seen, the higher brain and prefrontal cortex don't complete their development until around age 25. This is the part of the brain that helps you to make reasoned decisions, be logical, think through consequences and act with self-control.

The limbic system, which is responsible for your instant emotional reaction to events, is fully developed much earlier. This means that young people tend to experience strong and powerful emotions such as anger, sadness and fear, which can appear rapidly as 'mood swings'.

When you are experiencing strong emotions such as fear or anger, the limbic system can take control or 'hijack' your brain, making it more difficult for your higher brain to operate, so it's harder to think clearly or make balanced decisions. This is why it's often best to pause and take a breath before reacting when you are angry.

Risk-taking and peer pressure

In adolescence, you are also developing your sense of self – deciding who you are as a person and how you fit into the world. Because of this, it's common for young people to put a lot of energy and focus into being accepted by friends and peers, keep comparing themselves with others and be highly sensitive to embarrassment and the fear of being excluded socially. These concerns can all affect self-esteem and self-worth and can be amplified by social media.

Some young people are also drawn to risk-taking behaviour. This involves doing activities that have the potential to be harmful or dangerous. On first glance, this sounds bad! In fact, risk-taking is important, as it pushes us to have new experiences and challenge ourselves. We all need to take some risks to succeed in life, even if we can't be certain that things will go well or if we experience some uncomfortable feelings. We talk more about this in Chapter 8 on building confidence.

However, for some young people, problems occur because the limbic system of the brain is more 'in charge' than the more sensible and thoughtful prefrontal cortex. The limbic system gives us rewarding feelings from doing fun things – and these often include risky activities. This part of the brain is more impulsive and is not linked to careful or logical ways of thinking, so there is a greater chance of making riskier or unwise decisions.

Apply your GROW skills

The aim is not to avoid risk altogether, but to Follow your Guide and use your Wise Mind to make thoughtful decisions that encourage to you embrace challenge without taking unnecessary or extreme risks. If you are feeling strong emotions, there's a good chance that the limbic system may take over, leading to more impulsive choices, so you might need to use Open and Observe skills to help create a pause that allows you time to balance your emotions and invite your prefrontal cortex to get involved in deciding what's best for you.

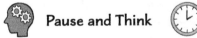 **Pause and Think** **5 Minutes**

Jyoti was studying for a history assignment. She read through the questions and started to answer them. At first, she was thinking clearly, and it felt good as she researched the questions and was able to give detailed answers.

Then Jyoti reached a question that she didn't fully understand. She wasn't sure what was being asked and she started to feel anxious and irritable. She began thinking, 'I'll never be able to do this! This question is too hard. Or maybe I'm stupid! I'll never get this done on time now!'.

Jyoti picked up her phone and noticed some messages on a group chat talking about the history assignment. 'I've finished it,' said her classmate, James. 'Me too — it was easy!' said another classmate, Eva.

Jyoti felt even more stressed. As her emotions started to rise, she found it even more difficult to focus on the difficult question and how to answer it. At this point, Jyoti's dad put his head round the door, 'Come on Jyoti, hurry up! Haven't you finished your homework yet? It's time for dinner.'

Jyoti's emotions exploded and she shouted back at her dad. 'You don't understand anything! This is impossible! I don't want dinner tonight!' She picked up the history assignment and ripped the paper into pieces and threw it on the floor.

Then she grabbed her coat and ran out of the front door.

Answer the following questions about which areas of the brain were involved in Jyoti's reaction.

→ At what point was Jyoti using her prefrontal cortex and her higher brain for thinking and reasoning?

→ When did Jyoti's limbic system (emotions) start to take over her thinking and decision-making?

→ At what stage did her brainstem and the survival system get involved?

→ How did worry about her friends affect the situation?

→ What types of impulsive or risky behaviour did Jyoti choose?

→ What other choices could Jyoti make in this situation? How could she use GROW skills to cope with this more effectively?

....

....

....

....

....

 **Read This**   **10 Minutes**

The three emotion systems

Another useful way to understand how the body and mind respond to stressful and threatening situations is to think about three different emotion systems. Each system has an important role to play in managing your emotional wellbeing and physical health.

The human brain has evolved to enable us to learn, develop incredible skills, imagine and create, and we can experience enormous thrills and joy. It also allows us to learn and solve complex problems in the physical world and to react quickly, to ensure we survive.

Unfortunately, this same problem-solving logic is less helpful for solving emotional problems, such as having unwanted thoughts or negative feelings, or dealing with stress. In fact, it can make the distress worse as your mind gets stuck in overdrive, repeatedly going over and over problems that cannot be solved by thinking or worrying. As we have already learned, strong emotions also affect your ability to use your higher brain for thinking clearly and can lead to you feeling overwhelmed by emotion as the limbic system takes over.

Let's take a look at a diagram of the three circles view of our emotion systems.

We will start by looking at each of the systems in turn, and then think about how we can keep all three systems in balance.

Threat system

The Threat system is your in-built survival system. It evolved to keep you alive and safe when in immediate danger and is controlled by the brainstem and a system of nerves that run throughout the body called the sympathetic nervous system.

The job of the Threat system is to alert you to any possible danger. By releasing hormones such as

adrenaline and cortisol, it tells your body to take immediate and instinctive action to keep you safe. This normally involves the 'fight or flight' reaction, where the body prepares to fight a danger or escape from it.

There is also a third survival reaction known as 'freeze', which can cause you literally to stay still – to avoid detection or prevent attention being drawn towards you.

The Threat system evolved when early humans were mostly having to face physical dangers, such as being threatened by a wild animal. It's important to act quickly in this situation; there isn't much time to think or plan what to do! So, the threat system can be triggered very quickly when your brain thinks you are facing any kind of danger.

We can explore the threat reaction using a CBT framework.

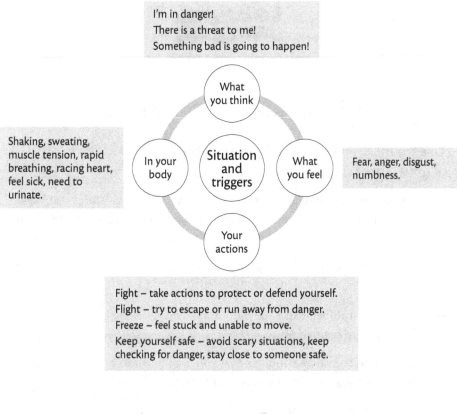

 Read This · 5 Minutes

THE HIGHS AND LOWS OF THE THREAT SYSTEM

The threat system is designed to cope with unexpected danger – and this is the system that will kick in to save you if you suddenly need to run out of the path of a speeding car to avoid being hit.

The downside is that for some people, the threat system can be oversensitive.

Our brains can overestimate risks and imagine or worry about threats that may not be real, are very unlikely to happen or are in the distant future when there's nothing you can do at this moment to protect yourself.

Spending too much time with an over-activated threat system can make you edgy, jumpy and unable to relax, and can get in the way of memory, learning and wellbeing.

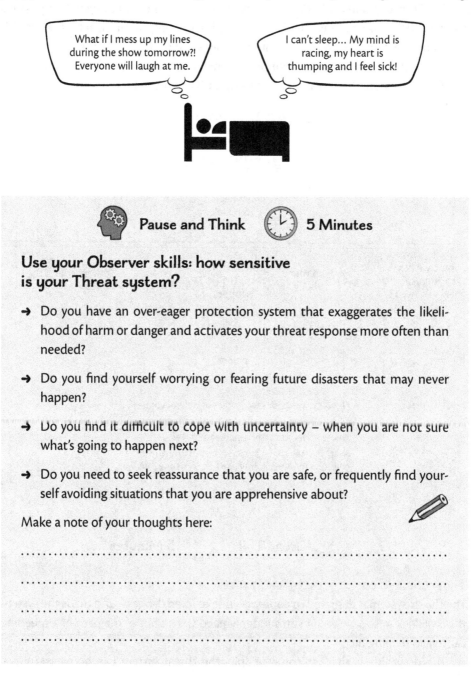

Pause and Think   5 Minutes

Use your Observer skills: how sensitive is your Threat system?

→ Do you have an over-eager protection system that exaggerates the likelihood of harm or danger and activates your threat response more often than needed?

→ Do you find yourself worrying or fearing future disasters that may never happen?

→ Do you find it difficult to cope with uncertainty – when you are not sure what's going to happen next?

→ Do you need to seek reassurance that you are safe, or frequently find yourself avoiding situations that you are apprehensive about?

Make a note of your thoughts here:

....

....

....

....

 **Try This** 🕐 **3 Minutes**

SOS SKILL FOR MANAGING THE THREAT SYSTEM:
GROUNDING IN THE PRESENT MOMENT

Use this whenever you need to create a pause and turn down the volume or sensitivity of the threat system.

1. Stamp or press your feet into the floor, and press your hands together or on the arms of the chair to **feel** where you are.

2. Look around the room and name in your head three things you can **see** around you.

3. Lower your gaze and notice and name three things you can **hear**.

4. Notice and name in your head anything you can **smell** or **taste** right now.

5. Describe all of these things in your mind as a sentence: 'I am sitting in a room with a chair, I can feel the back of the chair, I can hear the buzz of my laptop, I can smell and taste the toast I am eating. I am focused on the here and now.'

6. Now close your eyes and drop into your body, and take three slow breaths in and out from deep in your belly, noticing all the sensations inside.

7. Open your eyes and return to your activity.

We talk more about the threat system in Chapter 7 on anxiety and worry, and if you have a very sensitive threat system, this might be a helpful chapter to turn to next.

 **Read This** 🕐 **10 Minutes**

Drive and Achieve system

The Drive and Achieve system evolved to motivate us to seek out the things that we want or need to survive and thrive in life. This includes our need for food, shelter, friendships, treats and comfort. Our Drive and Achieve system is activated every time we pass an exam, win a competition or achieve any goal that we have set for ourselves.

When your Drive and Achieve system is activated, you get a small rush of excitement or pleasure, which is triggered by brain chemicals such as dopamine.

We can also explore Drive and Achieve reactions using a CBT framework:

I must get this completed or win!
I'm striving to achieve my goals...
If I persevere, I'll get this done...
I'm having too much fun – I can't stop!

What you think

A 'buzz' or a 'rush' – body feels activated and energised.
Can lead to craving, overstimulation, racing mind, difficulty relaxing.

In your body

Situation and triggers

What you feel

Joy, fun, excitement and pleasure if the goal is achieved.
Anxiety and frustration if goal achievement is blocked.

Your actions

Focus on completing activities and achieving goals.
Can lead to overwork and lack of relaxation.

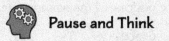 **Pause and Think**  **5 Minutes**

Using your Drive and Achieve system

→ Can you think of a time that you used your Drive and Achieve system to achieve something? What was this?

→ Can you remember how it felt to achieve this? What were your:

> thoughts

> feelings?

> What did you notice in your body?

> What did you do?

How does it feel to remember this achievement?
Make a note of your thoughts here:

. . . .

. . . .

. . . .

 **Read This** **5 Minutes**

THE HIGHS AND LOWS OF THE DRIVE AND ACHIEVE SYSTEM

The Drive and Achieve system is very important for getting things done! It helps keep you motivated and focused on accomplishing your goals, and this leads to a sense of self-esteem and pride when you look at your achievements. This is the system that enables you to meet deadlines, pass exams, develop new skills and take part and keep trying in sports and games.

But if you overuse the Drive and Achieve system, you can become over-focused and rigid about achievement, with a tendency to overwork. You might not allow yourself time to rest and recuperate and you might start to ignore other important parts of your life. Perhaps you work for hours into the night to prepare for exams, becoming exhausted, neglecting important relationships and forgetting to eat meals or take exercise.

The rush of excitement from achieving goals is very enjoyable, but this can become addictive. So, it's also important to keep a balance and remember to Follow your Guide, ensuring that your actions are taking you towards some of your most important and meaningful values and that you don't slip into 'overdrive'.

Overuse of the Drive and Achieve system can also make you overstimulated, causing problems with sleep, a racing mind and difficulty relaxing or winding down. And if your goals are blocked for some reason, you might experience feelings of anxiety, frustration and anger.

When you feel depressed or low, you might become demotivated or lose confidence in your ability to achieve goals, so you cut back on your usual activity and lose the sense of achievement from regularly activating your Drive and Achieve system. We talk more about how to overcome this tendency in Chapter 6 on low mood.

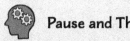 **Pause and Think** 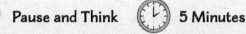 **5 Minutes**

Use your Observer skills on your Drive and Achieve system

Think about your personal patterns of using the Drive and Achieve system.

→ How active is your Drive and Achieve system? Do you find it easy to motivate yourself to set goals and make achievements?

→ Do you tend to overwork? Could you be relying too much on the 'dopamine rush' that arises with each successful achievement or win?

➜ Does this ever get in the way of enjoying your life and connecting with important people and activities?

➜ Or are you demotivated and lacking any sense of achievement, finding it hard to get started or keep going with tasks?

Make a note of your thoughts here:

....

....

....

....

Try This   3 Minutes

SOS skill for balancing the Drive and Achieve system: prioritise and plan today's to-do list

➜ Use your Guide to connect with your most important values today and how you wish to be as a person.

➜ Make a list of two or three things that are **important**, linked to those values, and that are also *urgent* (need to be completed today).

➜ Put a time frame on how long each priority task might take... Then add 10%  extra time to your estimate (things always take longer than expected!).

➜ Plan these tasks into your day for a specific time.

➜ Plan to do the task you least want to do first.

➜ Make sure you add in breaks and allow time for unforeseen problems.

➜ Notice how you feel after having taken 3 minutes to make this plan and to-do list.

Chapter 11 on Surviving Setbacks has some more tips on planning priorities and managing time.

Calm, Care and Connect system

The Calm, Care and Connect system evolved in mammals to allow us to rest and recharge when there are no threats to defend against and no goals that must be pursued. When this system is in operation, we feel soothed, peaceful and content, and we are motivated to nurture and care for ourselves and other people (and animals).

The Calm, Care and Connect system is triggered by 'feel-good' brain chemicals, including oxytocin, endorphins and opiates, and also involves a system of nerves called the parasympathetic nervous system.

We can explore the Calm, Care and Connect system using a CBT framework:

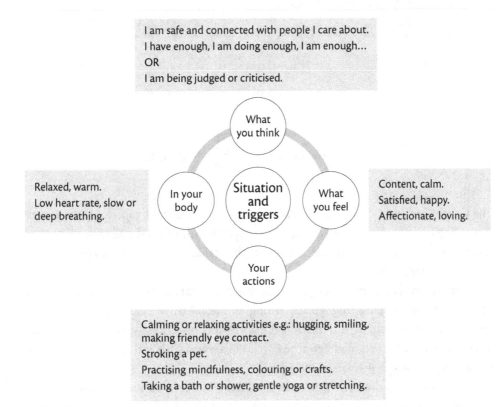

I am safe and connected with people I care about.
I have enough, I am doing enough, I am enough...
OR
I am being judged or criticised.

What you think

Situation and triggers

In your body

What you feel

Your actions

Relaxed, warm.
Low heart rate, slow or deep breathing.

Content, calm.
Satisfied, happy.
Affectionate, loving.

Calming or relaxing activities e.g.: hugging, smiling, making friendly eye contact.
Stroking a pet.
Practising mindfulness, colouring or crafts.
Taking a bath or shower, gentle yoga or stretching.

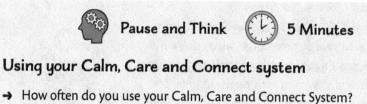

Pause and Think   5 Minutes

Using your Calm, Care and Connect system

→ How often do you use your Calm, Care and Connect System?

→ Do you regularly take time out for self-care and relaxing, soothing activities?

→ Are you regularly connecting with important and close people who you trust?

→ Is your to-do list too long or demanding, or are you allowing others to dominate or dictate what you do?

Make a note of your thoughts here:

....

....

....

Read This   5 Minutes

THE HIGHS AND LOWS OF THE CALM, CARE AND CONNECT SYSTEM

The Calm, Care and Connect system offers us a way to feel safe, calm and connected. Activating this system can help create a sense of contentment and wellbeing and offers protection and a way of recovering from the physical and mental stresses of living our challenging daily lives.

This system also helps us connect with those who care about us, bringing feelings of affection and helping to 'regulate' strong emotions as we spend time caring and being cared for by others. You might feel a sense of connection as you talk to a friend after a tough day. Or you might choose to relax in a warm bath and appreciate listening to calming music as a way of winding down.

Difficulties can arise if we don't use the Calm, Care and Connect system enough, especially when facing difficulties or setbacks, and this can lead to intense feelings of shame and self-criticism when things go wrong.

Problems can also develop if the Calm, Care and Connect system becomes linked to the Threat system. This can happen if those who are supposed to care for us are also frightening or abusive, so the behaviours and emotions that are usually linked to feelings of caring or safeness can trigger a sense of fear and threat rather than safeness.

An example of this could be if you misinterpret a friend's gesture of support when they offer to help you with an assignment, and feel angry or ashamed, thinking that they see you as stupid or incapable.

 **Try This** 🕐 **3 Minutes**

SOS SKILL FOR BALANCING THE CALM, CARE AND CONNECT SYSTEM

1. Take a deep breath in and hunch your shoulders to your ears. Breathe out with a deep, loud sigh from your mouth and drop your shoulders.

2. Reflect on things that have happened today or yesterday.

   > Find three things you can appreciate in the world around you, however small: 'My friend texted me, I noticed a flower, I like the feel of my cosy duvet.'

   > Now name one thing that you can appreciate in yourself or your actions: 'I helped with the washing up and my mum was pleased.'

 **Read This** 🕐 **5 Minutes**

The importance of kindness

We are much more likely to learn, use our higher brain powers and react in helpful ways to challenges if we feel understood and supported – living in a world where kindness is present. We cannot always control others or the situations or environments that we find ourselves in, but we can influence our own inner world. Building the skill of being kind to yourself is like developing a superpower that gives you strength and resilience when you are facing life's difficulties. You might start showing kindness to yourself by using some of the Open and Observe skills you learned in Chapter 3.

There are three aspects to kindness that are important for happiness and wellbeing.

→ **Being understanding towards ourselves**, especially when life is difficult and when we are coping with stress, life events or problems.

→ **Recognising that we are not alone**, we are humans and we are part of the wider world. Accepting that we are neither superhuman nor indestructible. Reaching out to others to give and receive support.

→ **Recognising our painful thoughts and feelings** in a balanced and non-judgemental way, without criticising or blaming ourselves or others. Learning to pause, step back, shift the focus of our attention and widen our perspective.

Strength through kindness

Kindness can be a source of hope and strength that helps you find the courage to Follow your Guide and create a life that you really care about. How can you find ways to develop your kindness superpower and to be kind to yourself as well as others?

Make a note of your thoughts here:

....

....

....

Balancing the three circles

Life is like a juggling act. To be healthy and happy, we must balance tasks, actions and priorities, and there needs to be balance and flow as the three emotion systems gently support each other. This is something that we have some control over. We can make active choices about our actions that will help to create more balance between the systems.

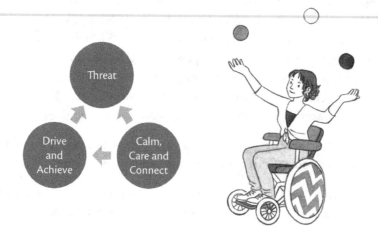

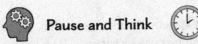 **Pause and Think** 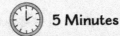 **5 Minutes**

How balanced are your circles?

Look at the three emotion circles above and imagine that they are balls you are juggling. Now think about the idea of balancing these systems and keeping up the rhythm and flow as you go about your daily life.

→ What might happen if one of the circles becomes too heavy, too large or too 'hot'? What would happen to the balance and flow?

→ Are your emotion systems in balance at the moment? Or do you spend a lot more time in one or two of the circles?

→ If they are not fully balanced, how does this affect you?

Make a note of your thoughts here:

....

....

....

....

 Try This 🕐 **10 Minutes**

Can you create more balance?

Think back over the past few days or weeks and answer the following questions.

What actions are you taking within each circle?

Complete the circles below with a list of actions that you are currently taking that relate to each circle. Try to include examples of actions that are both helpful and unhelpful, for example:

→ **Threat system**: Worrying about college work, avoiding assignments, checking my phone late at night.

→ **Drive and Achieve system**: Prioritising tasks and achieving them, setting ambitious time targets, aiming to run a marathon, over-promising, gaming until the early hours.

→ **Calm, Care and Connect system**: Taking time to chat to parents or friends about my day, switching off by taking a bath, stroking the cat.

What can you do more or less of to keep the systems more in balance?

→ Now add in some ideas to your circles of things that you may need to do more of, and strike out things you need to do less of.

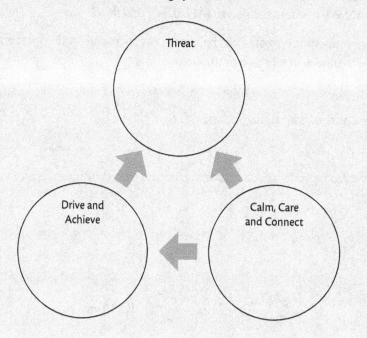

What we have covered in Chapter 5: Understanding your Brain and Emotions

→ Your amazing brain can change and GROW throughout your life, especially through finding ways to challenge yourself, participate in exercise and being creative.

→ There are three important parts of the brain that affect your emotions.

> The higher brain carries out thinking, planning, reasoning and decision-making. It doesn't fully develop until around age 25.

> The limbic system is responsible for emotions and memory and may

'hijack' the higher brain, leading to rollercoaster emotions and risk-taking actions and making it harder to think clearly or make plans and decisions.

> The brainstem controls your basic body functions and keeps you safe through the fight or flight reaction (threat response).

→ There are also three important emotion systems.

> The Threat system helps you react quickly and instinctively to keep safe from danger but may be oversensitive in some people.

> The Drive and Achieve system motivates you to take action and seek out the things you want and need, helping you get things done. Overuse can lead to overwork and exhaustion, whereas underuse can be linked with low mood and low motivation.

> The Calm, Care and Connect system enables you to feel safe and soothed and is important to recharge and rest. If it is underused, we can become self-critical or see others as threatening.

→ Kindness is a superpower that can provide strength and resilience when facing life's difficulties.

→ Finding a balance between the circles involves making active choices about our actions and finding flexible ways that allow each of the three systems to support each other.

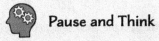 **Pause and Think**  **5 Minutes**

→ What are the most important messages for you from this chapter?

→ What have you learned or understood after reading it and trying the exercises?

Taking action

→ What are you going to do differently now?

→ What actions will you take as a result of reading this chapter?

→ Are there any regular actions or patterns of behaviour that you might try to practise or develop?

→ Which chapters in Part 2 will you turn to next?

....

....

....

....

....

....

BRINGING THE STEPS INTO YOUR LIFE

Chapter 6

BOOSTING YOUR MOOD AND MOTIVATION

→ Are you finding it difficult to see the funny side of things, enjoy life and see a bright future ahead?

→ Are you dragging yourself out of bed in the morning, feeling tired and saying to yourself, 'I can't be bothered to do much today'?

→ Does your mind churn over with negative thoughts, and are you spending more time on your own rather than with friends?

→ Do you want to lift your mood and find your mojo again? Read on...

 **Read This** **5 Minutes**

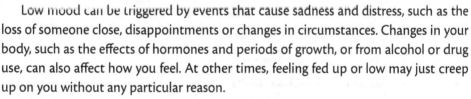

About low mood

Life is not an even path, and we all experience ups and downs in mood throughout daily life. But sometimes, things build up, and you might notice a pattern of feeling more fed up, low or demotivated than usual.

Low mood can be triggered by events that cause sadness and distress, such as the loss of someone close, disappointments or changes in circumstances. Changes in your body, such as the effects of hormones and periods of growth, or from alcohol or drug use, can also affect how you feel. At other times, feeling fed up or low may just creep up on you without any particular reason.

Feeling low for a prolonged period can cause changes in your thoughts, emotions and behaviour and have a major impact on your life if left unchecked. In this chapter, we will look at ways of overcoming low mood and boosting motivation, including how to:

→ use your Guide to find enjoyable and important activities that are likely to lift your mood and connect you to others

→ get Ready to take Action by setting realistic small goals to increase your enthusiasm and energy

→ being Open and Observing the moment, appreciating what's positive and unhooking from negative thoughts

→ use your Wise Mind to choose how to react, to plan helpful changes and to find ways to support, encourage and motivate yourself.

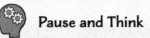 **Pause and Think** ⏰ **5 Minutes**

How is your mood?

Is low mood or lack of motivation starting to have a negative impact on your life? If so, it may be time to make some changes or seek some new ways to lift your mood.

Look at the list below and see how many of these possible signs of low mood are true for you.

Signs of possible low mood	Have you noticed this? Yes/No
You have been feeling down, depressed or low for at least a few weeks.	
You are more tearful than usual.	
You have strong or recurring feelings of boredom or apathy.	
You lack motivation and find it harder to start or keep going with important activities.	
You see yourself negatively and can be self-critical or blame yourself when things go wrong.	
You are no longer enjoying things that you used to find interesting or fun.	
You are finding it harder to concentrate than before.	
You are more irritable and intolerant of others.	
You are isolating yourself from friends and family.	
You feel tired and lethargic, no matter how much you rest.	
You are starting to think that the future looks bleak and that things may never improve.	

If you have ticked more than three or four of these items, you might need to think more about your mood and start looking for ways to make some changes. Keep going with this chapter for some ideas...

 **Read This** **10 Minutes**

When low mood becomes depression

We all experience occasional bad moods, feel fed up or act out at times, but it is important to recognise when low mood starts slipping into possible depression, with persistent or overwhelming feelings of unhappiness, lethargy or irritability.

Depression often goes unrecognised in young people, yet it can have a major impact on your life and ability to function, so it's important to spot it early and take action to overcome it.

Depression can lead to prolonged sadness or difficulty doing your usual activities. Maybe you find it harder to get out of bed each morning, so you stop going to school or work. Or you might find yourself withdrawing from your friends, not making eye contact or not chatting the way you used to.

For many young people, depression can also cause angry or irritable behaviour. If you find yourself getting into more trouble than usual or arguing with friends and family, this may be a sign that underneath you are feeling low or depressed.

When to be concerned

To help you decide whether your feelings are part of 'normal' teenage moods and emotions, or whether they indicate a more serious problem, you could ask yourself these questions.

→ How long you have been feeling fed up, irritable or low?

→ Are the changes having a major impact on your life?

→ How many of the above signs of possible low mood did you notice?

→ How much of the time do you feel down or negative? Do you have happier or more upbeat times, or are the negative feelings constant?

→ How differently are you feeling and behaving, compared to your usual self?

If you think you may be experiencing depression, we recommend that you visit your GP or talk to a trusted adult, such as a parent, teacher or older sibling. There are also many local and national support services available.

Thoughts of suicide

When you feel low or depressed, you may have thoughts about suicide or about not wanting to continue living. These thoughts can happen to anyone and having them does not mean that you will act on them. They will often pass as your mood starts to lift again.

However, having repeated negative thoughts about harming yourself is an important sign that you need support and care, so it's important to talk to someone that you trust. Talking about suicidal thoughts will not make you more likely to act them out, and sharing how you are feeling might help you find better ways to cope with difficult emotions.

If you are worried about suicidal thoughts, please seek help from your GP or a support line such as Childline or the Samaritans. At the end of this book, you can find links to some support organisations that you can turn to if you are struggling at the moment.

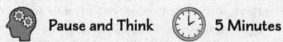 **Pause and Think** **5 Minutes**

What are the causes of low mood?
In the next section, we will look at some of the causes of low mood in young people.

Situations and triggers
Many life stresses and pressures can trigger feelings of low mood. Look at the following list and put a tick by any that are affecting you at the moment:

Stressful life event or situation	Is this affecting me? Yes/No
Problems at home (e.g. parents arguing or separating, difficulties with siblings)	
Financial or money worries	
Health problems (in you or someone you care about)	
Losing someone important	
Relationship problems or break-up	
Arguments or disagreements with friends or family	
Bullying (including online)	
Pressure to achieve (e.g. exams or other pressures at school or work)	
Problems affecting an important hobby or interest	
Any kind of physical, emotional or sexual abuse	

Coping with life stresses and problems

It's common to feel down when coping with life stresses, but if you start to feel over-whelmed or you are starting to see your problems as impossible to solve, this can have a negative impact on your mood, leading to frustration, anger and even thoughts of self-harm.

An alternative is starting to believe that you can cope with the problems that life throws at you. This can help to build your confidence and help to lift your mood. We talk more about this in Chapter 11 on Surviving Setbacks.

 **Read This** **10 Minutes**

CBT framework for low mood

When you feel low and fed up, you may also begin to view the world in a more negative way and behave in unhelpful ways that bring your mood down further. A CBT frame-work can be a helpful way to explore this, looking at how low mood leads to changes in:

→ thoughts – how you view yourself and the world

→ feelings and emotions

→ physical reactions in your body

→ what you do and how you react to the challenges of daily life.

Ignore the positives and see yourself and the world with 'dark-tinted' glasses.
Criticise and blame yourself for the slightest mistake.
Repeated gloomy thoughts about everything that's gone wrong.
Highly sensitive to criticism, rejection and possible 'failure'.

What you think

Low energy, feeling tired, even after rest.
Body feels drained and heavy.
Unexplained aches and pains, including headache and tummy upsets.
Effects of other physical health problems.

Sad, low, depressed mood.
Irritable, easily frustrated with angry outbursts.
Feel flat with less enjoyment of things you used to find fun.

What you feel

Situation and triggers

In your body

Your actions

Cut down socialising and pull away from friends and family.
Stop doing activities you used to enjoy, such as hobbies or sports.
Spend more time resting or staying in bed.

Pause and Think   5 Minutes

What did you notice?

Can you recognise any of these patterns of thinking, feeling and reacting to problems in your own life?

Make a note of anything important that you have learned here:

....

....

....

....

....

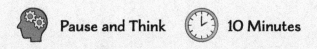 **Pause and Think** **10 Minutes**

Different reactions to the same problem...

To help you understand more about low mood, we will explore how two different people might respond to the same situation. See if you can spot which person is more likely to end up feeling fed up and low in these examples.

Example 1: No response to a text message

Kamila and Helen both text their friend, Rebecca, asking if she would like to meet up for a chat later in the week. But neither receives a reply that same day. How might they each react?

	Kamila	Helen
Thoughts	I knew she didn't really like me! What's the point in trying to contact anyone?	That's unlike Rebecca. I wonder if there is something wrong?
Feelings	Sad, fed up, annoyed.	A little concerned but calm.
In the body	Tired, headache.	Relaxed.
Behaviour	Turn off my phone and go in my room to watch TV alone. Avoid asking anyone else to meet up in future.	Chat to my mum about how I'm feeling. Give Rebecca a call tomorrow to check she's OK.
Impact of these actions	Feel more isolated, lonely and fed up.	Discover that Rebecca's phone wasn't charged yesterday and arrange to meet another time.

Imagine yourself facing a similar situation and ask yourself the following questions.

How would you interpret the situation – what thoughts would you have about it?

How might these thoughts affect how you feel?

What might you notice in your body?

What would you do?

What would be the impact of
these actions?
How might these actions affect
your feelings? Would they be
helpful or unhelpful?

Example 2: Football injuries

Let's look at another example. Milan and Daraz both love playing football but both have to miss a game because of an injury. They are both hoping to be picked for the football squad, but the coach decides not to allow them to play for another week. How might they react differently?

	Milan	Daraz
Thoughts	The coach thinks I'm useless at football. He'll never pick me to be in the team again. I'm such a failure.	I really wanted to play this week. What can I do to make sure I'm picked next time? I need to improve my game!
Feelings	Sad, hurt, hopeless.	Disappointed but determined.
In the body	Aching legs, tired.	Energetic.
Behaviour	Go home and don't turn up to the next training session. Spend all day playing computer games.	Train extra hard at home. At the next practice, I will ask the coach what I can do to get back into the team.
Impact of these actions	Lose confidence and skills. Coach may believe that Milan doesn't care about playing football.	Practise and improve football skills and show the coach his determination and commitment to the team.

Again, imagine yourself facing a similar situation and ask yourself the following questions.

How would you interpret the
situation – what thoughts would
you have about it?

How might these thoughts affect how you feel?	
What might you notice in your body?	
What would you do?	
What would be the impact of these actions? How might these actions affect your feelings? Would they be helpful or unhelpful?	

 **Read This** **10 Minutes**

Stuck in the Low-Mood Swamp

Feeling low can make you feel like you are stuck in a giant muddy swamp. Life feels difficult and your surroundings are grim. Your body feels achy and tired and even the smallest step is a huge effort.

It may seem like nothing will help and there's no way out. You might feel hopeless, and your mind may be telling you, 'What's the point? You won't enjoy anything, and you can't achieve much anyway!' So, you cut down your usual activities, which seem pointless and exhausting.

You stand still in the swamp, give up on trying to get anywhere and allow yourself to sink into the heavy, dark mud around you...

Giving up and reducing activity can make things worse

In real life, sinking into the Low-Mood Swamp tends to involve cutting back on things you used to enjoy and isolating yourself from other people. When you feel low, everything feels like an effort, and feelings of tiredness and difficulties concentrating make it harder to get involved and enjoy your usual activities.

You might also react by snapping at people, comfort eating or withdrawing into yourself and refusing to communicate. These actions may temporarily numb or distance you from difficult feelings but often lead to increased negative feelings as a vicious cycle over time.

In the short term, doing less might seem like it's helping, as you avoid having to make any extra effort when you are feeling tired and fed up. But the problem is that every time you avoid something, it gets even harder to do. It also means that you are missing out on opportunities to do things that you care about, and this tends to knock your confidence and mood even further.

And if you repeatedly turn down invitations from others, your friends and family may give up and stop involving you so much in their lives, leaving you feeling isolated and lonely.

So, as you can see, there are links between how you feel and how you react.

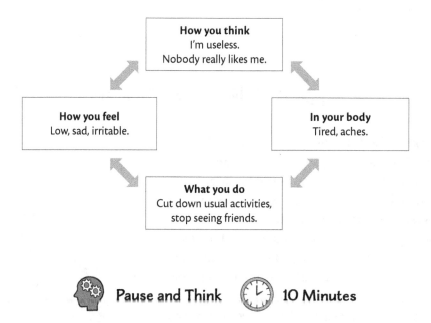

 Pause and Think   🕐 **10 Minutes**

BREAKING FREE FROM THE LOW-MOOD SWAMP

Aisha has recently broken up with her boyfriend Roshan. They were together for several years while at school, but then he had moved away to work for his uncle. They agreed that a long-distance relationship would not work.

Aisha and Roshan had shared many interests, such as badminton, dancing and walking. Although it was an amicable break-up, Aisha felt sad and missed Roshan's company, as he had been her partner in many activities. She found herself with time on her hands at weekends and most of her friends already had things planned, had different interests or had formed other friendship groups.

Aisha was invited to play badminton with a new partner, but she felt lost and apprehensive without Roshan and felt sure she would not enjoy it or would play badly, so she made excuses and didn't go. At first, after Roshan left, Aisha threw herself into her studies. But she started to feel exhausted and fed up and began making less effort. She could not shake off the sad feelings and her concentration got worse. She found herself staring into space in lessons, thinking about Roshan and how much fun he must be having in his new life without her.

Aisha started spending hours alone in her room, listening to sad music and sleeping late. She stopped coming down to have meals with her family and allowed her usually tidy room to get messy, with dirty cups and clothes all over the floor. She was snappy with her parents and became disorganised. She even had several rows with her sister, who was usually her best friend but who kept telling her to snap out of it and move on.

→ Can you recognise some of the things that need to change if Aisha is to get out of her Low-Mood Swamp, get back her motivation and improve her mood?

→ Is she Following her Guide? Is she Ready for Action? Is she using Open and Observe skills to focus on the present moment and make Wise choices and actions?

→ What are the good things that she knows about herself that she could use to start to turn her low mood around? Underline the key areas.

. . . .

. . . .

. . . .

 **Read This** **5 Minutes**

Improving your mood: plan your route out of the swamp

One of the best ways to start getting yourself out of a Low-Mood Swamp is to start walking really slowly and taking very small steps.

In real life, this involves 'behaving as if' you feel slightly better. This is based on a process known as behavioural activation, which has been shown to be effective in young people with low mood (Pass, Lejuez and Reynolds 2018).

'Behaving as if' means planning to do just a little more activity. This leads to a gradual increase in your energy and sense of achievement and lifts low mood.

You will probably still be feeling tired and fed up at first, and your mind may be telling you that this won't help and that nothing will make any difference.

But... you can take small steps anyway and see what happens! Eventually, as you keep walking, you might find that you have reached firmer ground. Your steps start to feel easier and your surroundings are nicer... and you are able to look up and spot an amazing view in front of you!

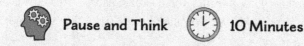 **Pause and Think** **10 Minutes**

Ask your Guide to help you plan activities

You can choose to do more of any activity at all, although connecting with people socially and physical activity are both effective for improving low mood.

The choice of possible activities is as broad as your imagination! You might decide to FaceTime with a friend, get out in the fresh air on your bike or skateboard or try practising your cooking and baking skills in the kitchen.

When deciding which activities to increase, it's helpful to ask your Guide about the people and activities that matter most to you.

Who and what is most important to you?

What has motivated you previously?

What are your core values? What kind of person would you choose to be?

If you could wave a magic wand and feel amazing tomorrow, how would this affect how you spent the day? What would you do differently?

What activities did you used to enjoy or do regularly in the past?

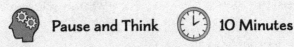

Pause and Think   **10 Minutes**

Balance your activities with SPICE

Try to make sure that your activities are varied and that they bring some **SPICE** to your day or week! This means that activities should involve the following elements.

→ **S**uccess or achievement.

→ **P**hysical activity and moving your body.

→ **I**mportant and meaningful to you.

→ **C**onnection or closeness to others.

→ **E**njoyable, relaxing and fun.

Here are some examples of many different types of activity. Put a tick against ones you might try. You don't have to try everything in one go! Add any of your own ideas and interests to the list.

Type of activity	Examples	What are your ideas and examples?
Success or achievement	Learn to touch-type Take an online photography course Try out a new recipe Sign up for an acting class Build a website Do the laundry Tidy your room Complete a project you've been putting off Learn a language Rearrange or redecorate your bedroom Write a poem or a short story Sort out your wardrobe Create a budget Make a to-do list Mow the lawn or do some gardening	

cont.

Type of activity	Examples	What are your ideas and examples?
Physical activity	Take your dog for a walk Go jogging or running Go for a bike ride Go swimming Jump on a skateboard or roller skates Do a yoga session Bounce on the trampoline Dance Practise your ball skills in football, tennis or basketball Learn to juggle Play frisbee golf Do a 10-minute workout Learn a martial art Go ice skating	
Important or meaningful	Start a podcast or a blog Volunteer for a local charity Do some shopping for an elderly neighbour Take your driving test Learn first aid Watch an online lesson Learn to change a lightbulb Find out how to do bike repairs Make a business plan for your next venture Apply for work experience Campaign for a change in the world Look for a job	
Connection or closeness	Join a book group or a choir Give someone a massage Play a board game Have a film night with friends Host a family quiz Make a card for a friend or grandparent Babysit for someone who needs a break Give your friend a makeover Cuddle your pet FaceTime a friend Tell someone a joke Write a letter Create a slideshow with photos of your favourite people	

Enjoyable, relaxing or fun	Learn to play guitar or piano
	Do a jigsaw
	Knit or sew
	Create a piece of artwork
	Practice mindfulness
	Go to the theatre or ballet
	Listen to music
	Have a home spa session
	Do a virtual escape room
	Get a new hairstyle
	Meditate
	Take a long shower
	Doodle, colour or draw
	Take a bubble bath
	Watch a comedy

 **Read This**   🕐 **5 Minutes**

 ## If you feel overwhelmed

If this all seems a bit like overload, don't worry! This is a common reaction to getting started in making any kind of change. Rather than giving up, try planning some super-small micro-steps. Think back to Chapter 2 where you learned about being Ready for Action.

When making life changes, one of the first steps is to build your confidence and belief that change is even possible. So, especially when you are getting started, it's better not to plan anything too challenging.

This is where micro-steps come in. They involve tiny changes, which are often so small that you think they won't make much difference or that change will be really slow.

Micro-steps don't necessarily fix a major problem, but they are a tiny step in that direction. They help to break ingrained habits and act as a reminder that you can make choices about what you do each day. They can get you started on the path to change and create a ripple effect that leads to improvements over time. Examples of micro-steps include:

→ going in the garden for 5 minutes to get some fresh air

→ finding your trainers in the garage and putting them by the front door

→ sending a short message to a friend to say hi.

Try This   **10 Minutes**

Choose a life area and then plan a micro-step that involves a tiny action that moves you in this direction. Use the planner below to help.

Planning micro-steps	Example	Complete your answers below
Choose a life area to focus on, using your Guide and a diary or SPICE tracker to help.	My education is important to me. I need to get started with a history assignment…	
What's one tiny step that moves you in this direction?	I will find my history book and put it on the desk.	
How long will the activity take? Aim for 5 minutes or less. Even one minute will help you get started!	5 minutes or less.	
How confident are you that you will do this in the next 48 hours? 1 = not confident at all 2 = a little confident 3 = so-so 4 = fairly confident 5 = I've got this – I will do it! Aim for a rating of at least 4 or 5.	3 – I'm worried I will forget.	
If your confidence rating is less than 4 or 5, what can you do to help? For example: lower the bar, make the goal easier or shorter, ask for help from someone, think about something you have achieved in the past to boost your confidence.	I will ask my friend to remind me as she is always very organised.	
What's the next small step towards your goal?	Next, I might plan to answer one question taking no longer than 5 minutes and have a break.	

You can download more copies of this planner from

Try This   10 Minutes

Activity diary
Why not try keeping a diary that keeps track of your daily activities?

Time	What was the activity? How long did you do it for?	Circle whether the activity is linked to 'SPICE' Success or achievement Physical activity or movement Important or meaningful Connection or closeness Enjoyment or fun	How was your mood after doing this (rate it from 1 to 10)?
7am		S P I C E None	
8am		S P I C E None	
9am		S P I C E None	
10am		S P I C E None	
11am		S P I C E None	
12 noon		S P I C E None	
1pm		S P I C E None	
2pm		S P I C E None	
3pm		S P I C E None	
4pm		S P I C E None	
5pm		S P I C E None	
6pm		S P I C E None	
7pm		S P I C E None	
8pm		S P I C E None	
9pm		S P I C E None	
10pm		S P I C E None	

You can download more copies of this activity diary from

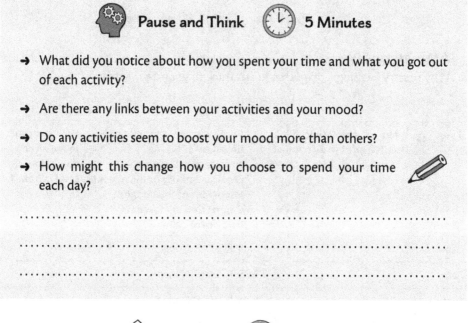

Pause and Think ⏱ **5 Minutes**

→ What did you notice about how you spent your time and what you got out of each activity?

→ Are there any links between your activities and your mood?

→ Do any activities seem to boost your mood more than others?

→ How might this change how you choose to spend your time each day?

....

....

....

Read This ⏱ **10 Minutes**

Keeping up the changes

After you try a new activity, it's useful to think about what you achieved and give yourself a pat on the back. Or, if for some reason it didn't happen, it's also helpful to think about why and if there is anything useful to learn from this. Chapter 2 has some useful checklists for reflecting and learning after you try a new activity.

And once you have made some changes to your life and hopefully started to feel a bit brighter, the next step is planning how to keep things going and avoid slipping back into the Low-Mood Swamp. Here are some tips for keeping up your positive habits.

CREATE A ROUTINE

Creating a routine can help you stick to helpful activities that will keep up a more positive mood over time. As your new patterns of activity turn into habits, it becomes easier to do them. Make sure your routine is flexible and can adapt to any new situations or events. We talk more about ways to create Healthy Life Habits in Chapter 10.

WRITE IT DOWN

Keeping a record of your activity levels using your phone, a diary or planner will help you to keep track of your achievements and can motivate you to continue making new changes. Take some time each week to look through your diary and check how you are getting on. This will help you to keep yourself on the right track.

Think about who could help or support you in planning and carrying out any of these changes, including friends, family, pets, your phone, your diary or an online community.

 **Read This** 2 Minutes

Roadblocks to getting out of the swamp...
Making gradual increases in your activity levels can lift low mood and increase energy levels but we know that making these changes is not always straightforward. Sometimes, negative thoughts or feeling tired, fed up or hopeless can get in the way of making changes.

In this next section, we will look at some of the thoughts and behaviours that can keep you stuck in the Low-Mood Swamp.

 **Read This** 10 Minutes

Do you ever slip into 'Bad-News Mind'?
When you are feeling low, you might notice that you have a more negative view of the world. You assume the worst and jump to the worst conclusions about yourself and other people. Your thinking can also get very stuck so you worry about the same things over and over again.

Remember the Unwanted Mind Visitors, the characters that sometimes invade your mind, bringing thoughts and messages that can stop you from doing things that matter to you, which we talked about in Chapter 4? You might like to take another look at that section to remind yourself (page 72).

When you are feeling low, it's often because several Unwanted Mind Visitors have shown up in your thoughts. These might include:

→ **The Pessimist**: Telling you it's all going wrong and there is no hope

→ **The Critic**: Telling you how useless you are and punishing you for mistakes.

→ **The Bone-Weary**: Telling you how tired you feel and how you just don't have energy to get anything done.

> You will have a terrible time if you go to the party... Don't bother – just stay home alone.

→ **The Mojo-Mugger:** Draining your energy and demotivating you.

→ **The Name-Caller**: Giving you a hard time and calling you names when things don't go to plan.

→ **The Blamer**: Unfairly blaming you for everything bad that happens.

→ **The Perfectionist**: Setting you impossible standards and only being satisfied if you are completely perfect.

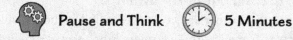 **Pause and Think** **5 Minutes**

Notice your Unwanted Mind Visitors

→ Do you recognise any of these negative visitors and how they see the world?

→ Do any of these visitors come into your mind when you are feeling low? Which ones visit most often?

→ What effect do they have on your mood and on your actions?

Make a note of your thoughts here:

....

....

....

 **Read This** **5 Minutes**

Coping with Bad-News Mind

So, how can you cope with these negative visitors and their unhelpful ways of viewing the world?

Start by remembering that these thoughts are not facts, and your mind is not always your friend. You don't need to listen to those characters or believe the unhelpful things they are saying to you.

Observe and notice when these negative characters have shown up in your mind. Just recognising they are there is the first step, allowing you to create a little bit of distance between your Wise Mind and these gloomy visitors.

 **Pause and Think** **10 Minutes**

Create your own 'Bad-News Mind' character

A helpful way to notice that the negative visitors are affecting how you are seeing the world is to create an image or a character that represents your mind when it's most negative.

Be as creative as you like! You might choose a downbeat or grumpy character from a TV show or a movie. Or imagine a cartoon creature or animal who has a really melancholy voice or outlook. Or maybe it's an angry character who gets frustrated and irritable with everyone around them.

If possible, try to be light-hearted and humorous with your ideas. Pick a character that feels right to you and matches how you see the world when your mood is low. Then ask yourself these questions.

What tone of voice would this
character have?

What kinds of things would the
character say?

What feelings or emotions would
it bring?

How would this character react to
problems or difficulties in life?

What would it tell you to do?

What would happen if you
followed this character's advice?
How would this affect your life?

 **Read This** **10 Minutes**

 A Wise alternative view

Can you remember the Wise Mind that we talked about in Chapter 4? The voice of your favourite coach, teacher or best friend, or maybe a combination of these!

Your Wise Mind can see when the negative visitors have come to call but doesn't necessarily agree with their negative point of view. Your Wise Mind can give you kind, caring and sensible advice about other ways to view the situation and believes that you are capable of dealing with the problems that you face.

Your Wise Mind doesn't need to get angry with the negative visitors or get into an argument with them. Wise Mind simply smiles and comes up with a different perspective...

Pause and Think   **5 Minutes**

→ What message would your Wise Mind give you when the negative visitors have come to call?

→ What advice would your Wise Mind give you?

→ How can you use your Wise Mind to help when you are starting to feel low?

Make a note of your answers here:

....

....

....

Read This   **10 Minutes**

Sinking into stuck thoughts

Do you ever get stuck in low-mood thought loops where you keep looking back at something that's gone wrong, going over it repeatedly in your mind? There might also be a 'gloomy glow' filter to your thinking so that you only focus on the parts of a situation that went wrong rather than having a balanced memory of how things were. Maybe one or more of the Unwanted Mind Visitors are affecting the way you remember what happened!

Getting stuck in low-mood thought loops often also brings a sense of low energy and lack of motivation to break free. Mojo-Mugger is a common visitor when you get stuck in loops of negative thinking, as well as many others. You might notice chains of thoughts like these...

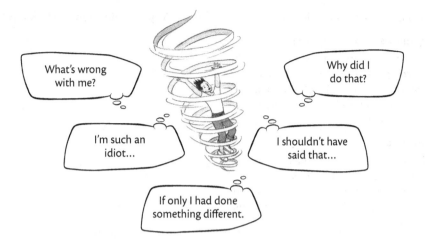

It's hard to break away from repetitive thoughts like these, which can seem to suck you into a downward spiral, but there are some skills that can help.

 **Try This** 🕐 **10 Minutes**

Take a look at the following list of ways to cope when you get stuck in a chain of negative thinking. What will you try next time this happens to you?

Step out of stuck thought loops	How can you use this? What will you try?
Observe and Open Notice that you are stuck in a negative thinking loop. Try using a five senses practice or 'notice and name' what you are experiencing to step out of the loop, and then move on to a SPICE activity with your full attention.	
Distract yourself Negative thinking loops often fill empty spaces and time when you are on your own or unoccupied. What activities could you try that take your energy and attention away from the Unwanted Mind Visitors and their negative thought loops?	

cont.

Step out of stuck thought loops	How can you use this? What will you try?
Use kindness as a superpower Being kind to yourself and showing yourself some compassion and acceptance can be important ways of breaking free from the self-criticism and self-blame that often come with low mood.	
Write it down Writing down how you are thinking and feeling in a journal or notebook can help to sort out what's going through your mind and start to make your thoughts and feelings more manageable.	
Use problem-solving If you can't stop thinking about a specific difficulty, problem-solving may help you find ways to cope with it. We talk more about this in Chapter 11.	
Talk to someone Talking to a trusted friend, adult or counsellor can help you get another perspective and make you feel less alone.	

 Try This   🕐   10 Minutes

I can't be bothered... managing low motivation

When your mood is low, it can be difficult to motivate yourself to make changes and hard to get past the negative thoughts and feelings that drain your enthusiasm and energy.

Maybe the Mojo-Mugger has come to visit, bringing gloomy messages about how nothing you can do will make things any better.

So, how can you overcome these negative messages? Here are some tips that can help to boost your motivation.

Motivation tips	How could you use this? What will you try?
Plan a mega-micro-step! Motivation has a snowball effect: if you start the ball rolling by doing something – however small – the change will gain momentum and become easier.	

Follow your Guide: Link your actions to your personal values. What is it about the activity that may make you feel good and want to do it? What are the benefits to yourself or to others?

Just DO IT! Don't keep waiting until you feel like doing something because that may never happen. Instead, just **do it** and watch how your motivation and mood catch up afterwards. Check the effects on your mood using the SPICE activity tracker (page 127).

Energise yourself with a short burst of activity, especially with boring tasks that make concentration difficult. Try 5 minutes of physical activity, have a quick shower or go into the garden and get some fresh air! What happens to your energy and mood? Follow this with a realistic plan for a few more minutes of the original task.

Ask your Wise Mind: What encouraging words would your inner coach or best friend have? What might be a kind way of helping you take action? Can you use this to motivate yourself?

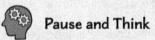 **Pause and Think** 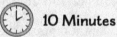 **10 Minutes**

Find your Good-News Story

It's also important to make an active effort to notice any small positive life experiences or things that have gone well rather than only focusing on what's gone wrong. Taking time to do this each day can help to counteract the negative visitors and their gloomy way of looking at the world.

Look for a Good-News Story	Example	What can you think of?
What do you appreciate right now, in this moment? Look around and find at least three things.	The sun is shining this morning and the sky looks beautiful. I had a delicious bagel for breakfast.	

cont.

Look for a Good-News Story	Example	What can you think of?
What are you doing in your life that Follows your Guide and takes you towards what is important? Choose small examples.	I love my dog and I take him for a walk every day. I messaged my friend because I knew she was upset, and she is important to me.	
Keep a good news diary, where you make a note each day of one or two small things that you can be pleased or proud of.	Toni said that my hair looked nice today! I got a good grade on my assignment.	
Celebrate your resilience! What challenges are you facing and what hurdles are you overcoming that you can feel proud of?	It's been hard to get over failing my driving test but I'm starting lessons again and I'm proud that I haven't given up.	
Pay it forwards! What small ways can you show kindness or appreciation to the people around you?	I thanked my dad for picking me up after my exercise class and gave him a hug.	

What we have covered in Chapter 6: Boosting your Mood and Motivation

→ We all feel low at times, and this includes feeling depressed, being tearful, struggling to motivate yourself and getting irritable and angry.

→ Being stuck in the Low-Mood Swamp means that you feel fed up and tired and everything seems like a huge effort, but cutting down your activities and stopping seeing people tends to make things worse.

→ In the swamp, you might meet many Unwanted Mind Visitors and thoughts that suck you in and keep you stuck in Bad-News Mind.

→ Getting out of the swamp involves taking small steps and behaving 'as if' you feel slightly better, which will gradually increase your energy and sense of achievement and lift your mood.

→ Add SPICE to your life by planning a wide range of activities that involve these elements: Success or achievement, Physical activity and moving your body, Important and meaningful, Connection or closeness to others, Enjoyable, relaxing and fun.

→ Micro-steps will make the changes seem more manageable and help prevent overwhelm.

→ Finding a Good-News Story by looking for something small that you appreciate or something that you are proud of can help create hope, shift your focus out of gloomy thoughts and lift your mood.

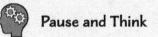 **Pause and Think**  **5 Minutes**

→ What are the most important messages for you from this chapter?

→ What have you learned or understood after reading it and trying the exercises?

....

....

....

Taking action

→ What are you going to do differently now?

→ What is the first micro-action that you can commit to trying?

→ What's the next chapter that you will turn to for more information and ideas?

....

....

....

Chapter 7

WORKING WITH WORRY AND ANXIETY

→ Are you feeling tense, on edge, nervous or irritable and finding it difficult to chill out?

→ Is your mind often in a whir of worry and 'what if?' questions, constantly picturing or imagining the worst possible scenarios?

→ Do you tend to bury your head and ignore problems or avoid situations so you don't have to face uncertainty?

→ Do you want to free yourself from fear overload and move forward? Read on...

 **Read This** **10 Minutes**

What is anxiety?

Anxiety is part of the normal human experience and will appear whenever we are facing something that seems scary or threatening, leading to worry, feelings of fear, nervousness and unease. This leads to changes in your body that alter how you think and behave and allows you to react rapidly, to keep yourself safe in the face of possible danger.

It's normal to experience anxiety if you are facing a stressful event, situation or decision, and experiencing a distressing or traumatic experience can also lead to anxiety about having to face a similar situation again.

The pressures of living in an uncertain world can also make us anxious, especially when the media tends to focus on negative events, with endless disturbing images and stories that can make the world seem hostile and frightening. Having constant access to information via the internet and computers brings many benefits but may also feel overwhelming and lead to increased anxiety if you find yourself checking this too often or comparing yourself unfavourably with others on social media.

But despite the bad press, anxiety is not all bad and can also be useful. The nervousness and fear that arise before sitting an exam or giving a public performance can keep your mind focused, encourage you to prepare and help you to perform on the day. So, the aim is not to get rid of anxiety altogether but to make sure it stays in balance and doesn't get in the way of fully living your life.

In this chapter, we will learn more about anxiety and take a balanced look at how to cope with worry and fear. This includes:

→ using your Guide to help you choose what's important and make sure that anxiety is not moving you away from the things that you value

→ being Ready for Action by planning small steps towards things that are important that you might be avoiding

→ using Open and Observe to manage uncomfortable thoughts, worries, feelings and sensations of anxiety, allowing you to step back and create some space so they feel less overwhelming

→ using Wise Mind to decide which thoughts are helpful and what Wise choices and actions you can take.

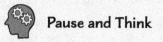 **Pause and Think** 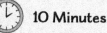 **10 Minutes**

Spotting anxiety

Anxiety can become a problem if it begins to affect or limit how you live your daily life, or if it gets in the way of important relationships with other people. Recognising when you are anxious is important, as it's the first step towards getting some help and there are effective treatments available. The sooner you start tackling anxiety, the better you will feel.

Take a look at the following checklist of possible signs of anxiety. If you notice more than three or four, this could be a sign that you need to think about some new ways to help you cope with anxiety.

Possible signs of anxiety	Do you notice this? Yes/No
Do you often worry about things before they happen?	
Do you find it difficult to relax and wind down?	

Do you suffer frequent physical complaints such as tummy
aches, headaches or muscle pains?

Do you often try to avoid situations that are likely to make you
feel anxious or worried?

Do you prefer to be with someone who will make you feel safer
or frequently ask for reassurance?

Do you have lots of worries about many different things, such
as friends, school, work or your hobbies?

Do worries or a racing mind often affect your sleep?

Do you often feel afraid that something really bad might
happen?

Do you seem to worry or get anxious about situations much
more than friends and family or people around you?

 **Read This** **10 Minutes**

Physical causes of anxiety

Drinking too much caffeine, eating lots of sugar, certain food additives, alcohol and
some drugs can all trigger anxiety. Some health conditions such as an overactive thy-
roid gland can also cause body reactions that may look like anxiety.

If you are concerned about your physical symptoms, we recommend visiting your
GP to rule out any medical or non-anxiety causes of your symptoms.

Different types of anxiety

There are many different types of anxiety. We won't talk about them in detail, but we
have given a brief overview of the most common types below. If you are concerned
that you might be suffering from any of these conditions, we recommend that you
talk to a trusted adult or visit your GP for further advice, as they can all be successfully
treated, especially when they are picked up early.

Panic attacks

A panic attack is a short episode of severe anxiety, which usually comes on quickly and
lasts up to around 30 minutes. The person has intense feelings of fear, and there may
be strong physical reactions, such as tightness or pain in the chest, sweating, dizziness
and choking sensations. Panic attacks can even be confused with a heart problem, as

the body sensations may be strong. People often begin to avoid activities that they fear may trigger a panic attack and this can have a major impact on daily life.

Generalised anxiety disorder (GAD)

People with GAD worry about many different situations and life problems. The worry is out of proportion to the problems and involves repeated loops of thinking about the same problems without planning how to cope or what to do. Worry often also affects the body, causing tiredness, headaches, muscle tension and difficulty sleeping.

Social anxiety

People who suffer from social anxiety experience fear in social or performance situations such as speaking or eating in public, going to parties, performing in front of others or talking to new or unfamiliar people. They may worry about appearing nervous or about making mistakes that mean they will be judged or rejected by others.

Obsessive-compulsive disorder (OCD)

OCD involves repeated unwanted thoughts, such as beliefs about danger, responsibility or the need for perfection, a fear of contamination from dirt or germs, or concern with order or symmetry. People with OCD also usually have overwhelming compulsions to repeat certain rituals or behaviours, such as frequent handwashing, counting or checking, to try to 'neutralise' the thoughts and reduce their distress. These thoughts and behaviours can interfere with the person's daily life and can affect educational and work performance

Body dysmorphic disorder (BDD)

People with BDD tend to worry about possible 'flaws' in their physical appearance, such as nose shape or skin problems like acne. The problem or difference is usually very small and may not even be noticeable to other people, yet it can lead to high levels of anxiety and avoidance of social situations. They often try hard to conceal or hide the flaw with clothes or makeup and may go as far as seeking unnecessary medical or cosmetic treatments for the problem, although this is rarely successful in reducing distress.

Post-traumatic stress disorder (PTSD)

PTSD can arise after exposure to an extreme traumatic event that causes intense fear or horror, such as acts of violence or severe accidents. After the event, people can re-experience highly distressing images and memories of the experience as flashbacks and nightmares. To prevent this, the person tends to try to avoid anything that reminds them of the past experience. They also become edgy and irritable, find it difficult to relax or sleep, and can become depressed.

Phobias

A phobia is an extreme fear of an object or situation, such as dentists, spiders, lifts or snakes. The fear is far greater than the actual danger or threat, and leads to sensations such as nausea, sweating, shaking and a fast heartbeat whenever the person encounters or even thinks about the object that they fear.

 **Read This** **3 Minutes**

Why do we have anxiety?

The purpose of anxiety is to help your body rapidly prepare for and react to any possible threat or dangerous situation. The body reactions that allow this to happen are known as the **fight flight freeze response**. You may remember this from Chapter 5 where we looked at the developing brain and your emotion systems, including the Threat response.

The Threat system has been present since early humans had to fend off wild animals in order to survive. To do this, they would have to **fight** off anything that was threatening, or take **flight** and run away, moving quickly to escape a dangerous situation, or **freeze**, so that they could not be seen by the prey. If the threat is real and you are in danger, anxiety is protective and ensures survival.

 **Pause and Think** **5 Minutes**

Imagine you are walking across a road that's usually very quiet with hardly any traffic. Suddenly, around the corner veers a huge truck. You realise that it's not slowing down! The driver beeps his horn loudly and you can hear the roar of the engine.

Without even thinking, you start running for the safety of the pavement, and after a few steps, you reach safety as the truck thunders past.

What sensations might you feel in your body?

 Read This   10 Minutes

The fight flight freeze response

The fight flight freeze response is activated by your sympathetic nervous system. The hormone adrenaline is released and creates an automatic survival response to help you deal with what you are seeing as a danger and a potential threat.

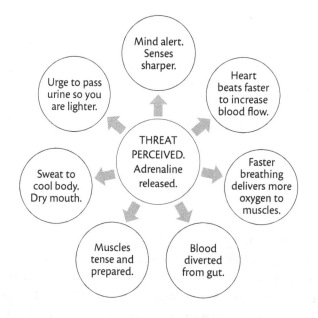

Because of these body changes, you can run quickly to the side of the road and escape being knocked down by the truck. You've survived!

But this surge of hormones can be intense and if it is not used as it is intended – to get you out of danger – or if it lasts longer than a few minutes, it can cause unpleasant sensations. You may get blurred vision, muffled ears or breathlessness, feel sick or dizzy, be unable to move or think clearly... and your mind can start to worry that something is seriously wrong with your health!

It is important to recognise that the body sensations of anxiety that you notice when your fight flight freeze response kicks in are **not** dangerous, even though they may be unpleasant. They are **normal** reactions to threat that help keep you safe and will gradually fade away once the threat has passed. Understanding this can be the first step in coping with anxiety.

 **Read This**  **5 Minutes**

The anxiety alarm system

Just like a smoke alarm, anxiety is an important system that alerts you and helps you keep safe in the face of threat and danger.

You can think of it like a smoke alarm. If there is a fire, you want the smoke alarm to alert you early, so that you can quickly take action to put out the fire.

Anxiety is less helpful if it happens too often, perhaps when there isn't any serious danger, or if it lasts for a long time, even after the danger has passed.

This is like having a super-sensitive or overenthusiastic smoke alarm. One that goes off as soon as your toast starts to brown, but well before it is burning! This can happen when we overestimate or exaggerate dangers and threats in our mind, leading to a stronger anxiety response than we really need to get us out of trouble.

Or perhaps your anxiety response doesn't quickly settle back down after the danger has passed, so you find it hard to stop worrying. This is like a smoke alarm that's hard to turn off once it starts beeping!

But we don't throw the smoke alarm in the bin if it goes off unnecessarily, because one day there might be a fire and we want to be prepared for this.

Likewise, we don't want to get rid of our anxiety response. Instead, when you notice feelings of anxiety, you can learn to check quickly for danger and then find ways to switch off the alarm and continue with your day, without letting it affect you for too long.

It's helpful to have an anxiety response that's roughly in proportion to the threat – so you can rely on it to sound if there is a fire and you can trust it to help get you out of danger when you need it.

But if on some days, it's a bit over-eager and goes off a bit too often, it's not the worst thing... you will cope!

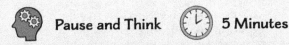 **Pause and Think** **5 Minutes**

→ How sensitive is your anxiety alarm? Does it go off more often than you need it to?

→ How easy is it to switch it back off again?

→ Does it sometimes go on for longer and spiral out of control?

→ What sort of situations, people and places often set off your alarm system?

→ Are your three emotion systems (Threat; Drive and Achieve; Calm, Care and Connect) in balance?

. . . .

. . . .

. . . .

CBT framework for anxiety

A CBT framework can be a helpful way to explore your anxiety reactions. Take a look at some of the common reactions when your anxiety alarm system is set off.

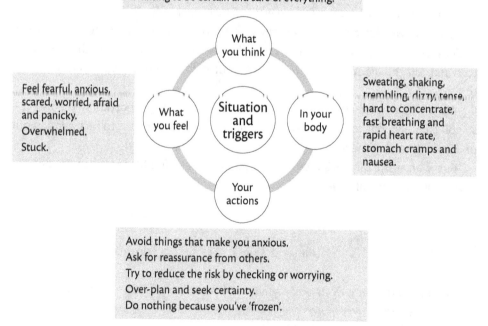

Exaggerate the problem in your mind.
Focus on everything that could go wrong.
Believe that you can't cope with problems or don't try to solve them.
Wanting to be certain and sure of everything.

What you think

Feel fearful, anxious, scared, worried, afraid and panicky.
Overwhelmed.
Stuck.

What you feel

Situation and triggers

In your body

Sweating, shaking, trembling, dizzy, tense, hard to concentrate, fast breathing and rapid heart rate, stomach cramps and nausea.

Your actions

Avoid things that make you anxious.
Ask for reassurance from others.
Try to reduce the risk by checking or worrying.
Over-plan and seek certainty.
Do nothing because you've 'frozen'.

Unwanted Mind Visitors in anxiety

When you are feeling anxious, it is common to experience changes in the way that you think and see the world. You might notice that many of the Unwanted Mind Visitors we talked about in Chapter 4 tend to pop up, causing feelings of anxiety, worry and panic. Common visitors who you may meet when feeling anxious include:

→ the Catastrophiser, who always jumps straight to the worst possible outcome in any situation

→ the Worry-Wort, who goes round in circles thinking over and over possible problems and achieving nothing

→ the Certainty Sergeant, who is rigid and controlling, and always wants to be sure what's going to happen and feel certain that nothing will go wrong.

These visitors bring terrifying messages of threat and danger and try to convince you that scary possibilities are more likely and that you are not capable of coping under pressure. They usually take a very negative view of the world and will tend to do the following things.

→ **Exaggerate the risks**: They assume the worst possible outcomes are more likely or more serious than they really are.

→ **Focus on what could go wrong**: They tend to pay more attention to what might go wrong and ignore what might go well.

→ **Convince you that you aren't capable of coping**: So you feel overwhelmed and don't try to work out how to deal with difficulties.

→ **Go round and round**: Anxious Mind Visitors are often very persistent and keep going on and on about risks so it's hard to think about anything else.

→ **Insist that you need more safety**: They might want you to carry out actions such as asking for reassurance or checking, which may work briefly in the short term, but often worsen anxiety and undermine your confidence in a negative spiral.

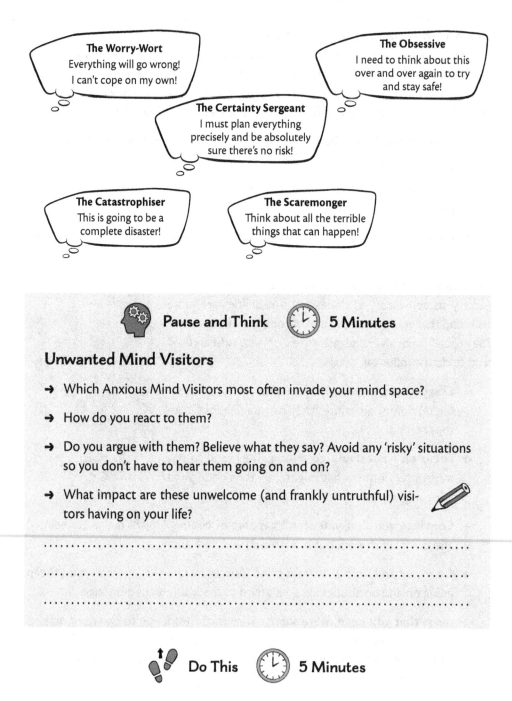

The Worry-Wort
Everything will go wrong!
I can't cope on my own!

The Obsessive
I need to think about this
over and over again to try
and stay safe!

The Certainty Sergeant
I must plan everything
precisely and be absolutely
sure there's no risk!

The Catastrophiser
This is going to be a
complete disaster!

The Scaremonger
Think about all the terrible
things that can happen!

Pause and Think   **5 Minutes**

Unwanted Mind Visitors

→ Which Anxious Mind Visitors most often invade your mind space?

→ How do you react to them?

→ Do you argue with them? Believe what they say? Avoid any 'risky' situations so you don't have to hear them going on and on?

→ What impact are these unwelcome (and frankly untruthful) visitors having on your life?

....

....

....

Do This   **5 Minutes**

STOP Anxious Mind Visitors

Try this STOP activity next time you notice that any Anxious Mind Visitors have paid you a visit!

1. Spot the struggle and Stop what you are doing.

2. **T**ake a breath from deep in your belly and exhale as slowly as possible.

3. **O**bserve your thoughts and feelings, using labelling to recognise that the Anxious Mind Visitors are around: 'Hello Scaremonger! I see you, Worry-Wort.' But don't get involved in a long conversation or try to reassure or convince them (or yourself) not to worry.

4. **P**roceed by focusing your attention on the here and now rather than the future! This means choosing whatever activity is most important and doing it with your full attention. Use your five senses to connect to the activity fully: vision, hearing, touch, smell and taste.

The endless roundabout of worry...

Anxious thoughts are common and often involve unanswerable 'what if?' questions about the future. Our minds can invent the worst possible outcomes and exaggerate or 'catastrophise' about the risks we are facing. There is a lot of questioning, doubting and seeking answers to things we are not sure about.

Anxious thinking often involves a specific type of thinking known as worrying. Worry is like a never-ending circle of thinking about things that might go wrong but which does not solve the problem.

We all worry sometimes about specific situations, events or challenges in our lives, but too much time spent worrying can get in the way of living and lead to feelings of stress, anxiety and low mood.

Worry is another type of survival skill that humans have developed to allow us to use our imaginations to think ahead and plan how to cope with possible danger before it even happens. This helps us to keep safe and prevents things from going wrong.

But not all problems can be solved by thinking them through, especially things that are in the future. So, we may get stuck on the Worry Roundabout, going endlessly round the same problems, over and over again. And this is when worry becomes unhelpful and can take up a lot of time and energy.

'What if?' thinking

Worry tends to involve imagining possible future problems and often starts with a 'what if?' thought. These can be linked in rapid chains of worry about all kinds of different possibilities.

→ What if... I look silly in front of my friends?!

→ What if... I make a mistake in the exam?!

→ What if... I get sick?!

→ What if... I make the wrong decision?!

 **Try This** ⏰ **5 Minutes**

Test out your 'what if?' predictions

The Anxious Mind Visitors often get involved in worry! The Catastrophiser will tell you that things will almost certainly go wrong... but how often is that actually true? How can you find this out?

Try writing down what you fear or anticipate will happen in a notebook or journal. Then look back afterwards and find out if the worst really did take place!

Most of the time, you will discover that the majority of your anticipated fears never come true. And if they do, you can cope!

 **Read This** ⏰ **5 Minutes**

Anita had a tendency to worry about the worst possible outcome in every new situation she faced or every event she was invited to. One day, a friend invited Anita to take the train into the city to go shopping together, but Anita's mind was full of worries and Anxious Mind Visitors, who kept saying things like: 'What if we miss the train coming back? What if we get lost? What if we lose our purse? Maybe we could even get kidnapped!'

Anita was close to her mum and they talked often. Her mum was very kind and patient while talking things over and kept reassuring Anita that nothing bad would happen. This helped for a short while, but the Anxious Mind Visitors kept coming back, and Anita kept on needing reassurance over and over again.

Anita thought about staying at home to avoid the worries, but she was starting to feel left out — she really wanted to spend time with her friends and have fun.

Anita also asked her older brother about some of her worries, but he had a different approach and didn't reassure her. He too was patient and listened, but when she asked for his advice or for reassurance, he replied by asking her some questions instead.

- *What exactly are you worried might happen?*

- *Realistically, how likely is it that the problem will actually happen? Is it very likely or is it more that the Scaremonger or the Worry-Wort are talking?*

- *How important is it to you to go on this trip? What direction is your Guide pointing in?*

- *If things did start to go wrong, what could you do to cope or solve the problem?*

- *What helpful things does your coach tell you in netball training? Can you ask your 'inner coach' for some advice?*

Her brother suggested she make a note of her answers on her phone, so she could look at them again if she started to feel anxious and he was not around to prompt her.

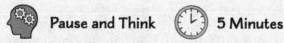 **Pause and Think** 🕐 **5 Minutes**

→ What was the best approach for Anita – her mum's reassurance and avoiding events, or her brother's questions that encouraged her to think of ways to cope?

→ How could you use this approach on something you are worrying about?

→ What questions could you ask yourself? What helpful coping phrases could you write down to remind yourself?

Make some notes here:

....

....

....

GROW your skills to cope with anxiety and worry

There are many different GROW skills that you can use to cope with anxiety and worry. The choice will depend on the situation that you are facing and the type of worry that you are experiencing.

 **Try This** **5 Minutes**

Quick tips for coping with anxiety

The best action to help move you away from intense feelings of anxiety or repeated worry thoughts can depend on how your body is feeling. You might need to release tension or calm and soothe yourself.

If you are very tense with an excess of pent-up energy, a short burst of intense exercise might help release this, as long as it is not just before you are winding down to sleep. Try sprinting on the spot, skipping, jumping or any kind of high-intensity activity. These can help bring your emotions down and take your mind away from worry thoughts.

Or, if you are exhausted or just feeling agitated and restless, you might need to calm, cool and soothe your emotions with a warm bath, a splash of cool water on your face or a few slow breaths or try stroking a pet or watching something relaxing.

Can you experiment with different ways of coping with anxiety and worry for different situations? Which ones do you find most helpful?

 **Read This** **5 Minutes**

Follow your Guide and face your fears

Many of the body sensations that come up when you feel anxious can be pretty uncomfortable, yet many of these can also appear with pleasant emotions, such as excitement. Could those butterflies in your stomach or that tingling in your muscles be telling you that you are about to embark on something important or exciting? Could you see it as an adventure rather than something to be frightened of?

In Chapter 8 we look at building confidence, which may involve taking yourself outside your Comfort Zone. When you can cope with these body sensations, you might be able to take an important step in the direction of what matters to you!

Remind yourself of your Guide and your most important values. Who and what are most important to you and how do you wish to be as a person? Do you want the Scaremonger or Worry-Wort to dominate your personality and spoil your life chances and fun?

Ask yourself **why** you are doing things – what meaning they have for you and what purpose? Following your Guide may involve facing your fears, new situations and uncertainty, but it may be worth it in the pursuit of what matters. You could use the voice of the Guide to create some useful coping phrases and reminders.

 **Read This** 🕐 **5 Minutes**

Avoidance and other Away Actions

The actions that we choose to help cope with anxiety are often aimed at reducing or preventing feelings of anxiety and worry. You might try to avoid people, places and activities that make you feel anxious, even if you know they are important. Procrastinating, or putting off getting started with things, is another type of avoidance that may also be linked to feelings of anxiety.

When the Anxious Mind Visitors show up, you might also do things to make yourself feel safer, such as asking for reassurance from friends and family. Repeated checking is also common. So, if you are worried about your health, you might start looking up information on the internet about the possible causes of your symptoms or checking your body for possible illness.

These reactions might help you feel less anxious in the moment, but do they help in the long run?

Unfortunately, avoiding important things that are scary or uncertain, constantly asking for reassurance and over-checking are all Away Actions that move you away from your Guide and the things that you care about. And they also tend to undermine your confidence and create a negative spiral of increasing anxiety over time.

📖 **Read This** 🕐 **5 Minutes**

Taylor really wanted to pass their upcoming exams to get onto an engineering apprenticeship course. The mocks were coming up in four weeks and they knew they had to get down to some solid revision.

Taylor had a churning feeling in the stomach every time they thought about sitting in the exam room, but rather than using this as motivation to revise, they had become very good at doing everything else except start the revision. They had even tidied their bedroom and helped with mowing the lawn!

To make more time to study, Taylor cancelled tennis practice, which they normally found energising, enjoyable and stress-releasing. They made a strict revision timetable that filled the daylight hours, but they found themselves just sitting there, staring into space and worrying about failing the exams. The revision just wasn't happening.

As the situation got worse, Taylor began to worry about it at night. To keep their mind off the exams, they started playing games online in the evenings but found this created a rush of excitement that made it hard to stop playing and get to sleep.

Things were spiralling out of control and time was running out. Scary images kept coming to mind of getting to the exam room and having nothing at all to say. Taylor was losing sleep, didn't want to get up in the morning and was starting to invent excuses about feeling ill to avoid going to school.

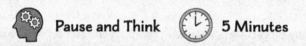 **Pause and Think** 🕐 **5 Minutes**

Taking steps towards what is important

→ What helpful coping strategy had Taylor stopped doing that might help release some tension and stress? What could they do right now to get things back on track?

→ What was the effect of late-night technology on Taylor's fight flight freeze response? What could they try that might be more helpful?

→ How could Taylor break down the revision into smaller steps so it was not overwhelming and difficult to get started?

→ What help could they enlist or what resources could they use?

→ How could Taylor gradually build up to going into the exam room?

→ What would be the first micro-step?

....

....

....

....

....

 **Read This**  **5 Minutes**

Ready for Action: approach rather than avoid

Taking steps towards coping with scary situations may mean finding manageable ways to approach rather than avoid your fears. But you don't have face your worst fears all at once or get overwhelmed by stress and anxiety.

Facing a fear is a bit like climbing a ladder – especially when you are concerned about heights. You don't have to rush to the top, and if you did, you might feal queasy!

Instead, choose a firm footing for your ladder, take one small step at a time and maybe even enlist a helper to hold the ladder in place and encourage you or give support until you feel steady. You might need to pause and take a breath with each step to make sure your ladder does not wobble and to take in the lovely view from where you have reached!

Imagine getting to the top and how you might feel when you accomplish this, even if it seems difficult to face right now. Imagine enjoying what you see from the top of your ladder, and congratulate yourself.

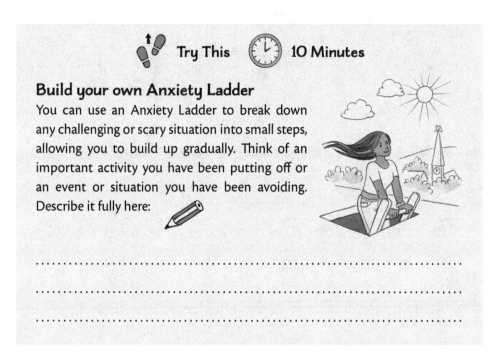

Try This **10 Minutes**

Build your own Anxiety Ladder

You can use an Anxiety Ladder to break down any challenging or scary situation into small steps, allowing you to build up gradually. Think of an important activity you have been putting off or an event or situation you have been avoiding. Describe it fully here:

....

....

....

What resources do you have and what help can you seek out that will help make sure you have a firm footing and some support?

. . . .

. . . .

. . . .

Now create your own ladder – like the chart below – leading up to your challenging situation at the top of the ladder. Draw at least five to ten rungs – or small steps – up the ladder to move you towards your challenging situation. For each step, make a note of the answers to these questions.

→ What will you try?

→ When and where will you try it?

→ Who or what can help you achieve this step?

→ What skills can you use to help you successfully cope?

Remember, you can get help at each stage, or pause for a moment and repeat a step before moving up to the next rung.

 Now go for it – one step at a time. It will be worth the effort!

You reached your goal!!

↑ **Step 6**

You nearly made it...! What can you try next?

What will you try?

When and where?

Who and what can help?

What skills can help you cope?

↑ **Step 5**

Don't give up... how can you stretch a little higher?

What will you try?

When and where?

Who and what can help?

What skills can help you cope?

↑ **Step 4**

Keep going – look how far you have come!

What will you try?

When and where?

Who and what can help?

What skills can help you cope?

↑ **Step 3**

What's the next step?

What will you try?

When and where?

Who and what can help?

What skills can help you cope?

↑ **Step 2**

What's next – can you step up the challenge a little?

What will you try?

When and where?

Who and what can help?

What skills can help you cope?

↑ **Step 1**

What could be an easy first step?

What will you try?

When and where?

Who and what can help?

What skills can help you cope?

 Read This  5 Minutes

Wise Mind

Wise Mind can help you make helpful choices about what to do and how to cope when you start to feel anxious. It is also about choosing to listen to your inner coach and Following your Guide rather than listening to some of the Anxious Mind Visitors who pop in uninvited.

Are these Anxious Mind Visitors helpful and taking you towards things that are important or matter to you in life? Or are they taking you away from valued life directions? Are they keeping you stuck in a loop going nowhere?

 Read This 5 Minutes

Use a revolving door

You don't have to talk back, argue or even listen to the Anxious Mind Visitors. Think of them coming in and out through a revolving door! Just give them a nod and acknowledge them by name as the come in and go out: 'There's the Catastrophiser,' 'OK Worry-Wort,' 'Hey Scaremonger....'

There is no need for them to hang around; just set the revolving door to auto, and allow them to wander back out of your mind when they are ready!

And sometimes they might have an important point to make, so you can press pause, make space to listen to what they have to say and then let them wander off when you've had some time to think it through.

You could also invite your inner coach to come in through the door, take a seat and stay for a while, so you get a Wise perspective on all the different thoughts and points of view...

 Try This 5 Minutes

Look at the big picture

Worry and anxiety often make us have a very narrow view of things – like tunnel vision. You can get fixated on all the worrying parts of a situation and miss all the enjoyable and interesting bits. Or perhaps you are forgetting about all your skills, strengths and abilities!

Next time you are thinking about a situation that is making you anxious, try thinking about the following things.

→ **Is this helpful?** Is the way you are thinking helping you to be the person you want to be and to do the things you care about?

→ **Can you take a helicopter view?** Imagine yourself rising above the situation so that you can see **all** sides from a distance. How does this change things?

→ **Look at the big picture**: How would others see this?

→ **Take the test of time**: How will you see the situation in a week, two weeks or six months ahead?

→ **Let go of certainty**: Can you be more relaxed and willing to accept not knowing what is ahead? It could be exciting, adventurous, spontaneous and thrilling!

Then focus on **now**. Don't try to stop or control your thoughts, just put them on the 'back burner' – let them simmer quietly and focus on an important task you need to get on with. Why not turn back to the 'Pay attention to daily activities' or 'Using your five senses' sections in Chapter 3 and try out focusing on your daily activities or using your five senses to 'drop anchor' and come out of worry thoughts and back into the present moment.

 Listen to This   5 Minutes

5-MINUTE WARM WELCOME

This clip helps you to open up to uncomfortable experiences using breathing and mindfulness to observe and step back.

 **Read This** **5 Minutes**

Use a worry decision tree

You can use a worry decision tree to help you cope with worries. This involves deciding whether a worry is something that you have some control over and you can take some action on, or whether it's just something that **might** happen or that you cannot control.

If you can do something about the worry, you can use problem-solving to think about what action to take and then make a plan to carry out this action at a specific time. We talk about this in Chapter 11 on Surviving Setbacks.

If you can't do anything about the problem right away, or the worry is about something that you can't really control, you might need to shift your focus.

 **Try This** **5 Minutes**

Allow a worry to come into your mind and think about it for a minute. Now use this tree to ask yourself the following questions.

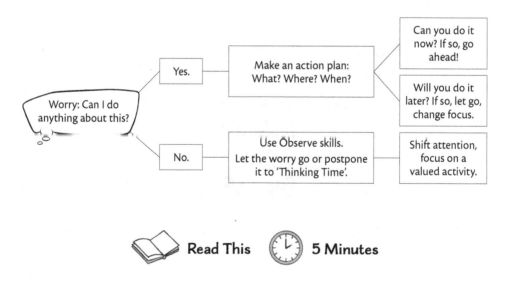

 **Read This** **5 Minutes**

Put worry 'on hold' with 'Thinking Time'

Thinking Time is a way of coping with too much worrying. It involves choosing when you want to allow the Anxious Mind Visitors time to have their say. Sometimes, they may have something important to contribute!

But we don't want them chatting all day and getting in the way of you living your life. So, it's helpful to choose some time to think about your worries and concerns. But rather than doing this throughout the day, choose a convenient regular time to think through any worries or problems you are facing.

If worries pop into your mind at other times, you can choose to put off worrying or put it 'on hold' until your planned Thinking Time.

 **Try This**   **10 Minutes**

Plan your Thinking Time

Use these steps to plan out your daily Thinking Time.

Step 1: Plan your Thinking Time: Choose a slot of 15–30 minutes for Thinking Time each day, ideally at the same time and in the same place, and preferably not just before bedtime.

Step 2: Put the worry 'on hold': If a worry pops into your mind at another time of day, tell yourself: 'It's OK to have this worry, but I will deal with it later. I'm going to put off thinking about it until Thinking Time.'

You can make a note of any worries or problems you want to remember in a journal or your phone. After writing it down, close the book again until Thinking Time.

Step 3: Focus on your daily life: After noting down your worry, close the book, focus your attention back on the present moment and concentrate on whatever activity you are carrying out. This will help to let go of the worry until Thinking Time arrives later on.

Don't be concerned if the same thought pops back again very quickly. It is common to have repeated worry thoughts. Just repeat the same process: accept the thought, write it down and put it on hold for later.

Step 4: Allow your Thinking Time: During Thinking Time, you can look through your list of worries or problems.

Cross anything off the list that is no longer a concern. Now it's time to think about these problems as much as you like!

If you can, use problem-solving skills from Chapter 11 on overcoming setbacks to help you cope with any practical problems.

Continue your Thinking Time for a maximum of 30 minutes. Then, move on to another activity that is likely to take your mind away from your worries and lift your mood, such as exercise, listening to music or calling a friend.

What we have covered in Chapter 7: Working with Worry and Anxiety

→ Anxiety is designed to help your body rapidly prepare and cope with any possible threat or dangerous situation through the fight flight freeze response. This reaction can be very uncomfortable but is not dangerous, although it can become a problem if it begins to limit how you live your daily life.

→ Anxiety often involves Unwanted Mind Visitors such as the Catastrophiser, the Scaremonger and the Worry-Wort, who will try to convince you that scary possibilities are more likely and that you are not capable of coping under pressure.

→ You don't have to listen to these Anxious Mind Visitors and can let them wander back out of your mind through a revolving door! Recognising that thoughts are fears not facts and are unlikely to happen, 'surfing' the worry, coming into the present by 'noticing the now' and finding ways to cope can also help.

→ It's also helpful to cut down on anxiety actions such as avoidance, reassurance and checking, which reduce the range of activities you enjoy, make you withdraw from people and reduce confidence.

→ Using your GROW skills will help you cope with anxiety and worry. So, Follow your Guide, be Ready for Action and take small steps up the Anxiety Ladder, Observe and don't get intimidated by what you fear, make Wise choices and free yourself from the Worry Roundabout.

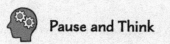 **Pause and Think** 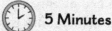 **5 Minutes**

→ What are the most important messages for you from this chapter?

→ What have you learned or understood after reading it and trying the exercises?

....

....

....

Taking action

→ What are you going to do differently now?

→ What actions will you take as a result of reading this chapter?

→ What will you practise on a regular basis in order to build on what you have learned?

....

....

....

Chapter 8

CREATING CONFIDENCE
TO BE YOU

→ Do you find it hard to believe in your own abilities, or do you lack confidence in yourself?

→ Do you avoid challenges because you don't think you can succeed?

→ Are you too self-conscious to try new things for fear of making a fool of yourself?

→ Do you want to feel more confident and accepting of who you are? Read on...

 Read This   10 Minutes

What is confidence?

Having confidence involves believing in yourself and your abilities. It's not about being arrogant or seeing yourself as superior to others but about knowing inside that you can achieve the things that matter to you. Confidence is also related to self-esteem, which includes feeling good about yourself and believing that you're a worthwhile person.

When you feel more confident, it's easier to make decisions and choices that are right for you. But having confidence doesn't mean that you can't make mistakes. In fact, sometimes we can learn much more by making a mistake and changing how we do things the second time around. Confidence also arises from being kind and accepting yourself – acting like your own best friend – when life is challenging or when things are not going according to plan.

It's usually easier to try to **behave** with confidence rather than to **feel** more confident. This means it doesn't matter if you sometimes feel anxious or have some inner doubts. Many people seem confident on the outside but doubt themselves inwardly.

So, you can never judge how confident another person feels just by looking at them. Developing confidence involves letting go of unhelpful comparisons and not judging yourself harshly against others.

Confidence can help you to get back on track rather than giving up when things get tough. By stepping forward rather than retreating after a setback, you can start to feel more confident to tackle challenges and deal with obstacles. We talk more about this in Chapter 11 on Surviving Setbacks.

Why confidence matters

Confidence can help you to feel ready for whatever life throws at you, encouraging you to get involved with new and exciting opportunities rather than backing away, avoiding challenges or giving up when things get tough, so you will be more likely to reach your full potential and succeed in the long term.

The good news is that you can learn to GROW your confidence with time and practice. This may involve being willing to 'give things a go' without giving yourself a hard time if you don't succeed first time, and also finding ways to cope with any uncomfortable thoughts and feelings that pop up when you are feeling less confident.

In this chapter, we will use the 10 Minute GROW approach to:

→ Follow your Guide by making confident choices that are in line with your personal values

→ stretch outside your Comfort Zone and increase your skills and confidence

→ choose confidence-boosting rather than confidence-draining activities to move you into the Performance Zone

→ recognise and build on your own qualities and past successes

→ cope with any self-defeating or critical thoughts that undermine your confidence.

 **Read This**  **5 Minutes**

Guide yourself towards confident choices

Confidence comes from within and from knowing who you are and who you would like to be. It's hard to feel confident about yourself, what you are doing or how you are doing it if these things are not a good 'fit' with who you really want to be and what you care about most.

This is where your **Guide** comes in, the inner compass that helps you keep focused on what matters to you most in life. What did you discover in Chapter 1 about your values and the direction you wish your life to take that might affect your confidence?

You can also GROW your confidence by making choices that Follow your Guide and allow the 'real' you to shine and contribute to the world. Let others see you for who you really are – including any mistakes, insecurities and imperfections – rather than concealing these or acting in a way that's not really true to you.

Pause and Think   5 Minutes

Ask your Guide about confident choices...

If you are not sure whether a choice or decision is Following your Guide, try asking yourself these questions.

→ Does this choice fit with your values, culture, personality and the personal qualities you would like to develop?

→ Will you find what you are choosing to try enjoyable, rewarding or meaningful?

→ What is the most important part of this situation for you? Why does this matter?

→ Will this move you towards a goal that's important to you?

Read This   5 Minutes

Get ready to take confident actions

Taking action with confidence is another important first step to GROWing your confidence. You can choose confident actions, even if you are having feelings of anxiety, worry, uncertainty and doubt. And by behaving 'as if' you feel more confident, alongside your worry or self-doubt – bringing these thoughts and feelings along for the ride – you may find that you start to feel more confident too. And even if your feelings don't change, by acting with more confidence, you are more likely to achieve the things that matter to you.

Acting with confidence involves:

→ putting in time and effort to develop your skills and knowledge to achieve goals or take part in activities that you care about or want to improve at

→ trying new experiences and new ways of doing things

→ taking part in challenges such as tests, performances and competitions

→ communicating with confidence using both words and body language

→ learning and developing based on constructive feedback

→ problem-solving and using your inner skills and strengths to handle problems or obstacles.

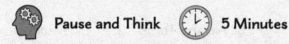

Pause and Think   **5 Minutes**

Take a look at the following list of actions and tick the ones that involve confident actions. Can you add any examples of your own?

Action	Is a confident action? Yes/No
Make eye contact and smile when you meet someone new.	
Stare at the ground and hope that no one notices you.	
Try a new activity even though you are not sure whether you will be good at it.	
Refuse to try something new in case you make a fool of yourself.	
Walk away from a situation that you know is not really safe or sensible.	
Get pulled into doing something that you later regret because you don't want to upset your friend.	
Give up at the first obstacle with a new project.	
Shout back at your tutor or sulk if you get some negative feedback.	
Refuse to give up, knowing that if you keep trying things will most likely get better.	
Sneer or make fun of people who don't get things right.	
Only doing things that your friendship group are doing or approve of.	
Giving up a sport if you don't win the competition you entered.	
Other ideas	

 Read This   🕐 3 Minutes

Practice makes perfect

One of the best ways to gain confidence in any activity or life skill is by gaining more experience in it. So, if you would like to get more confident in your ability to speak clearly in front of a group, you need to practise this. You might need to put in some time and repetition before you start to see your skills developing, but if you stick at it, you will start to improve and your confidence will naturally grow as well.

If you are struggling to see any improvement with practice, you might need to work on your resilience skills or use feedback from others to find out what might help you to learn and grow in this part of your life. We cover this more in Chapter 11 on Surviving Setbacks.

 Read This   🕐 10 Minutes

Stretch your confidence: step outside your Comfort Zone

One way to build your confidence is to challenge yourself to do things that are just outside your normal Comfort Zone. Let's look at some of the different confidence zones:

The Comfort Zone: Staying within your Comfort Zone feels very safe and secure! It's where life feels cosy and easy and there are very few challenges. This is great for resting and relaxing, but you could get stuck in a rut and miss out on opportunities if you spend too long here.

Getting **stuck** in the Comfort Zone often involves restricting your life and only choosing activities that you can already do with little thought or effort. It can be quite boring and rigid and can make you fearful of change. And by constantly avoiding things that you fear, your confidence and self-belief can shrink still further.

The Stretch Zone: As you gradually take small steps outside the Comfort Zone, you start to move into the Stretch Zone. Here, you are starting to take a few small risks and try some new things. You are more willing to experiment with life, test out what happens when you make changes and learn from your experiences. As you move into the Stretch Zone, you find that life starts to change and new possibilities begin to open up in front of you. And your confidence begins to grow as you start to recognise that you are capable of rising to new challenges. You are starting to say, 'Yes I can try this!'.

The Growth Zone: As you move into the Growth Zone, you are fully committed to trying new things, learning new skills and developing new abilities. You are willing to take an even bigger step away from the Comfort Zone towards an important goal.

Your confidence remains high in your own ability to learn and adapt to the challenges that you are facing. In this zone, you are also using your ability to bounce back from setbacks or obstacles as you draw on your inner confidence to keep going by looking for solutions and finding new pathways to your own successful outcomes. The Growth Zone is also where you start to get really skilful at what you choose to do.

The Overload Zone: In the Overload Zone, you have taken on a challenge that feels a little too overwhelming and difficult. If this happens, your confidence can take a dip, you may start to feel stressed and anxious and your performance might drop. It's wise to try to avoid reaching the Overload Zone when setting challenges and goals – to maximise your chances of success and keep your confidence high. But if you do reach this point, it's not a disaster. Simply recognise what has happened and drop back down into the Growth Zone or the Stretch Zone. You don't have to retreat all the way back to the Comfort Zone as this can get in the way of making progress towards your goal.

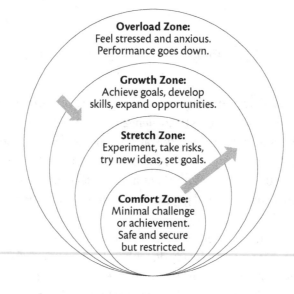

 Pause and Think **5 Minutes**

Confidence-boosting and confidence-draining actions

Another way to build confidence is to participate in more activities – and you don't have to wait to feel more confident before getting started! Ask yourself: **What would you do differently if you felt more confident?** Can you do some of these things anyway? Behaving 'as if' you feel more confident can help to build your confidence over time.

What actions or life choices could act as **confidence boosters** by moving you into the Stretch Zone and the Growth Zone? Which actions or choices will act as **confidence drainers**, zapping your confidence and moving you back towards the Comfort Zone? These choices will be different for all of us. They will also depend on the situation, the activity, the people you are with and the things that you enjoy or feel comfortable doing.

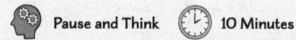 **Pause and Think** **10 Minutes**

Take a step outside your Comfort Zone

There are many ways to stretch your confidence! Think about where your Comfort Zone is now and challenge yourself to do something that's just beyond what you might normally choose. Pick something you'd like to do if only you had a little more confidence. You might decide to volunteer for a new project, sign up for a committee, try out for a team or a talent show, raise your hand and ask more questions, take a risk and talk to someone new...

Now, give yourself a nudge forward and give it a try!

Be kind to yourself, as taking the first step may be difficult or scary. To help motivate you, Follow your Guide and pick something that you genuinely care about. Take a look at this list of activities, which might help to give you some ideas. Can you commit to trying at least one new thing within the next few days?

How to stretch your confidence	Examples of confidence stretching in action	What might YOU try?
Stretching or improving one of your existing skills	I like tennis and I'd like to try playing someone new. I love cooking and I'd like to try a new recipe.	I will...
Learning or developing a new skill	I've never done public speaking before... I could join an acting group or a debating club.	I will...
Expressing your own ideas and opinions	I'm going to share my love of reading by joining a book club and telling others my views of a particular book. I'm going to put my hand up and answer questions more in my study group.	I will...

cont.

How to stretch your confidence	Examples of confidence stretching in action	What might YOU try?
Trying new hobbies and interests	I've always wanted to learn about coding... photography... car engines... singing... I'm going to join an online course or a local group.	I will...
Taking the lead by organising or running things	I'm going to stand for class representative or volunteer to take the lead in making a change at my workplace.	I will...
Feeling more in control by planning, tidying and organising	I will organise my bedroom or my wardrobe the way I like it. I will plan my schedule to make sure I can fit in all the things that are important to me. I'll keep an eye on my finances so I can save up for something that I really want.	I will...
Using your knowledge	I have knowledge about plants... sports... DIY... fixing things... I will take on a bigger project or learn something new, or find a way to share my knowledge with others.	I will...

Once you have tried your first confidence-boosting activity, pick something else to try. Do you want to build on this first step or try something completely different? Keep repeating this same process. Confidence grows with every step forward.

 **Read This** **5 Minutes**

Observe – what's getting in the way of taking confident actions?
The next step will help you to recognise and cope better with any uncomfortable thoughts and feelings that may undermine your confidence and lead you to avoid challenges and opportunities.

Explore confident actions with a CBT framework
We can use a CBT framework to help you find ways to move outside your own Comfort Zone and increase your personal levels of confidence. Here are some examples of how different experiences in each part of the framework might act as a block to choosing confident actions and stretching outside your Comfort Zone.

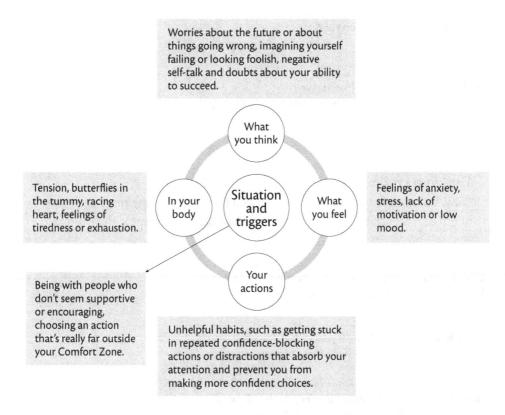

Worries about the future or about things going wrong, imagining yourself failing or looking foolish, negative self-talk and doubts about your ability to succeed.

What you think

Tension, butterflies in the tummy, racing heart, feelings of tiredness or exhaustion.

In your body

Situation and triggers

What you feel

Feelings of anxiety, stress, lack of motivation or low mood.

Your actions

Being with people who don't seem supportive or encouraging, choosing an action that's really far outside your Comfort Zone.

Unhelpful habits, such as getting stuck in repeated confidence-blocking actions or distractions that absorb your attention and prevent you from making more confident choices.

Pause and Think   **10 Minutes**

Use a CBT framework to explore your confidence-blocking reactions

Choose a situation in which you felt anxious, lacked confidence or felt stuck. What were your reactions?

Describe the situation: What was happening? When was it? Where were you? Who else was there?

Thoughts: What went through your mind? What were you thinking? What memories, ideas, stories or images came to mind?

In my body: What physical or body sensations did you notice? How did you feel in your body? What was your posture/body language like?

Feelings: What emotions came up?

Actions: What did you do? How did you
behave? Was there anything that you avoided
doing?

Building on your successes
Now, pick a different activity that you feel (even a little bit) more confident
about or have achieved (even a very small) success in and repeat this exercise.

Describe the situation: What was happening? When was it?
Where were you? Who else was there?

Thoughts: What went through your mind? What were you
thinking? What memories, ideas, stories or images came to
mind?

In my body: What physical or body sensations did you
notice? How did you feel in your body? What was your
posture/body language like?

Feelings: What emotions came up?

Actions: What did you do? How did you behave? How did
you behave differently to when you lacked confidence?

Final step: What's the difference?
Try to notice any differences between your reactions on
these two occasions.
How does lacking confidence affect your thinking styles,
your emotions and your behaviour? How does this change if
you feel even a little more confident?

What can you learn from this exercise? Make a note here...

....

....

....

....

Listen to This   **4 Minutes**

BREATHING WITH CONFIDENCE

Listen to this short audio clip of a breathing exercise to build your sense of confidence.

Read This   **5 Minutes**

USING GROW SKILLS TO MOVE ZONES

Jarred was preparing for his first attempt at public speaking as class represent-ative at a Year 12 staff and student consultation. He felt comfortable speaking to his classmates but nervous in front of the staff. But he wanted to get some practice in negotiating, as he was interested in marketing and sales as a career.

Jarred asked his friend Robert to help him build his confidence. Robert said he believed Jarred would do a good job and Jarred accepted the compliment. He practised his voice volume, posture and speech with several friends and listened to their feedback on how to cope with any questions or challenges — including ones that might make him feel uncomfortable or angry.

Before the meeting, Jarred felt nervous and had some negative thoughts that made his stomach churn and affected his breathing: 'The staff don't like me and will say I'm useless and won't listen to me. I will let the class down. I can't do this!'.

Jarred noticed what was making him uneasy and acknowledged that this was his first attempt at speaking to a large group. This was a big step outside his Comfort Zone! He paused and used some deep belly breaths to steady himself. He pictured how pleased he would feel and the sense of accomplishment from getting involved and standing up for his classmates.

He took a deep breath and decided to give it a try, telling himself that he had no evidence that the teachers did not like him or would judge him negatively.

In the meeting, he remembered what he had practised and was able to be clear and say what he wanted. He made Wise choices about how to answer ques-tions. He stood up for his class and explained the need to create some space in the busy timetable, even though he felt anxious when speaking.

By the end, Jarred was able to negotiate some extra study time for his year group before their mock exams — all without raising his voice or storming out of the room! He was congratulated by his year head and his classmates.

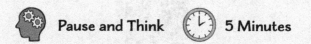

Pause and Think   **5 Minutes**

→ Which zone was Jarred in at key points in the story (Comfort, Stretch, Growth or Overload Zone)?

→ Which GROW skills helped Jarred cope with this challenge?

....

....

....

....

....

Read This   **10 Minutes**

Step into the Performance Zone

Finding ways to cope with difficult emotions is essential to performing, achieving goals, learning and enjoying life. We learned in Chapter 5 that strong emotions such as stress, anxiety and anger can affect your ability to think clearly and logically, making it harder to be creative or use your unique skills to the best of your ability.

Most of us perform at our best when we feel supported and encouraged by others and when we use kindness and positive motivation to cope with problems and difficulties. We also tend to perform better as we move into the Stretch Zone and the Growth Zone, where we feel inspired and motivated, and can move towards our goals and maximise our ability to learn and grow.

If you take on too much, have too much pressure or are overly critical of yourself, or if the environment is highly stressful, you are likely to tip into the Overload Zone. This is when your performance, abilities and enjoyment reduce, and you become less effective. This is true for all humans, so you are more likely to be a supportive friend or partner and a good leader if you find ways to show kindness to yourself and others.

PERFORMANCE

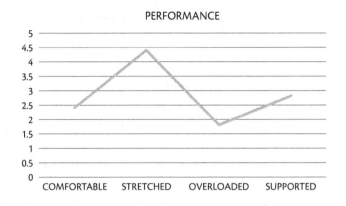

| | COMFORTABLE | STRETCHED | OVERLOADED | SUPPORTED |

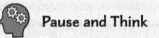 **Pause and Think** **5 Minutes**

Motivate yourself with kindness

Think of a situation in which you would like to stretch yourself a little and move out of the Comfort Zone and into the Stretch or Growth Zones.

→ How could you use kindness to yourself to create resilience and help motivate you to make these changes?

→ What attitudes or phrases could you use?

→ What kind actions could you take that would encourage you to be brave and embrace change, to grow your confidence?

→ How does it feel to motivate yourself with kindness rather than criticism or blame?

Make a note of your thoughts here:

. . . .

. . . .

. . . .

. . . .

. . . .

 Try This  **10 Minutes**

Make confident choices

It's important to notice when a lack of confidence is affecting how you are living your life. You can then decide to make Wise choices that help you achieve important goals. You might need to make these choices even when life seems uncertain or your confidence is a little shaky.

Stepping outside your Comfort Zone can often feel scary and uncertain. It might bring up difficult feelings such as fear, anxiety or doubt. You might notice some uncomfortable body sensations, such as butterflies in the tummy or tension in the chest or back, or feel your heart thumping in your chest.

This is where you have a **choice**. You can choose to try to avoid these uncomfortable feelings by staying stuck in the Comfort Zone. Or you can be willing to experience a little discomfort and choose to Follow your Guide and step into your Stretch Zone. And you can use mindfulness and Observing skills to help you cope with any uncomfortable feelings, which will often fade as you build your confidence.

 Pause and Think  3 Minutes

Use your Observe and Open skills

What Observing or mindfulness skills might help give you the courage to step outside your Comfort Zone? You might like to flick back to Chapter 3 for some ideas.

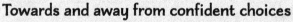

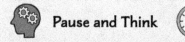 Pause and Think  10 Minutes

Towards and away from confident choices

Think about a situation in which you lack confidence. Pause for a minute and imagine yourself in this situation, about to take a risk or try something new. Ask yourself these questions.

→ What uncomfortable thoughts, beliefs, feelings, sensations or urges are taking you **away** from stepping outside your Comfort Zone and stretching your confidence?

→ What could you Open up to and be willing to experience in order to stretch outside the Comfort Zone and increase your confidence?

→ What small actions could you take that would start moving you into the Stretch and Growth zones?

....

....

....

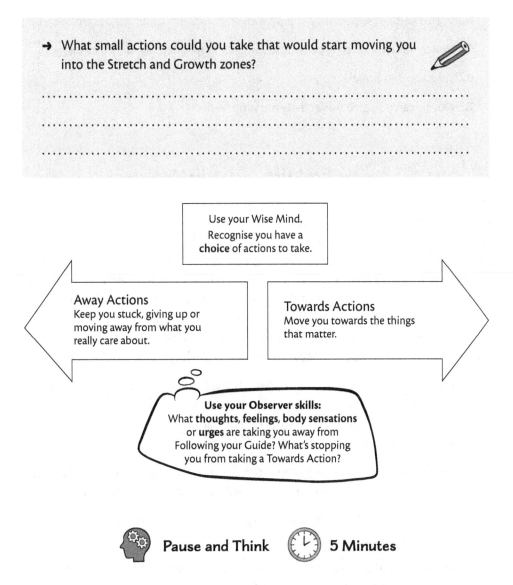

Use your Wise Mind.
Recognise you have a
choice of actions to take.

Away Actions
Keep you stuck, giving up or moving away from what you really care about.

Towards Actions
Move you towards the things that matter.

Use your Observer skills:
What **thoughts, feelings, body sensations** or **urges** are taking you away from Following your Guide? What's stopping you from taking a Towards Action?

Pause and Think   **5 Minutes**

Use your Observer to step outside the Comfort Zone

1. Imagine yourself taking a step outside your Comfort Zone. Visualise yourself doing something that will build your confidence and take you into the Stretch and Growth Zones.

2. If any difficult feelings arise, pause and take three slow breaths. Notice that you are able to cope and that you have enough space inside to hold all the difficult feelings and to continue doing the confidence-boosting activity because it's so important to you.

3. Then see yourself continuing to try this new activity and stretch your confidence and skills.

4. Watch yourself successfully coping with any problems or difficulties that pop up.

5. Watch yourself keeping going and not giving up when faced by a challenge.

6. Take another breath.

7. Now... can you give this activity a try in real life?

 **Read This** 🕐 **10 Minutes**

Wise Mind: create a Confident Mindset

Confidence can stem from our inner conversations and stories we tell ourselves about who we are and what we are (or are not) capable of. It's difficult to make the most of your life when you are constantly talking yourself out of going for the things you really want. And it can be frustrating and discouraging when you are constantly plagued by doubts, negative thoughts and fears about things going wrong.

A Confident Mindset involves looking at the world in ways that help to build your confidence to achieve important goals. There are many ways to help build this.

→ **Focus on your next step**: Look towards the future and think about what the next small step towards your goal might be. It sometimes helps to picture the outcome in your mind – a strategy used by famous sports people honing their goal-scoring skills.

→ **Be willing to take (small) risks**: Look for ways to step out of your Comfort Zone, take some risks and experiment with new ways to live your life.

→ **Have a 'can-do' attitude**: Believe that you can achieve success through time and effort. We talk about this GROWth Mindset more in Chapter 11.

→ **Show yourself kindness**: Be understanding, as if you were trying to build the confidence of one of your best friends.

→ **Focus on your strengths and cut down on negative comparisons with others**: By recognising **your** abilities and **your** potential, you will have far more opportunities to succeed. We are all different, so let's celebrate this!

→ **Keep at it**: It's essential to keep trying when life is filled with challenges and obstacles – allowing yourself to be resilient and to bounce back after mistakes and problems.

 **Read This** 5 Minutes

Recognise your qualities

Acknowledging your strengths and skills, any personal accomplishments and the qualities that make you unique is an important part of increasing your confidence.

When you receive a compliment, do you accept it with thanks? When you achieve something or something goes well, do you take time to notice and feel proud? Or do you tend to brush off or minimise praise and success, saying, 'Anyone could have done that' or 'It was nothing'?

You can grow your confidence if you allow yourself to acknowledge and absorb any positive feedback from others or acknowledge success when you achieve anything, no matter how small. Ignoring or minimising the good things that people say about you will have a negative impact that damages your confidence.

So, next time you receive a compliment, try smiling and saying a simple 'thank you'. It's also important to feel a sense of pride in your own talents, strengths, achievements and qualities. The next exercise will give you a chance to practise this.

Pause and Think 10 Minutes

What are your talents and personal qualities?

Use the questions in the following exercise to create a list of your own good points. Has someone ever told you that you're smart? Funny? Kind? Artistic? A caring friend? A good student? A talented writer? A promising athlete?

This might feel a little uncomfortable at first, as most of us are not used to dwelling on our own qualities. But this is about building your confidence by seeing the real you – it's not about being vain! If you find it difficult, you can also ask a supportive friend or relative for help.

Question	Now it's your turn...
What do you like about yourself, however small and fleeting?	
What are your positive qualities?	

cont.

Question	Now it's your turn...
What challenges have you faced? What personal strengths allowed you to do this?	
What gifts or talents do you have?	
What skills have you learned or developed?	
How might someone who likes and cares about you describe you?	
What do other people value in you? (Tip: Try asking a caring friend or family member what they think!)	
What qualities and actions do you most value in others? Do you ever show any of these qualities?	
Who do you most admire (e.g. a historical figure, celebrity, film or book character)? What qualities do you most admire in them that you can notice in yourself or that you could work towards?	

Confidence-blocking thoughts and stories

Think back to Chapter 4 on Wise Mind and the Unwanted Mind Visitors that can enter and try to dominate your thoughts. Does the Critic show up and drain your confidence when you are faced with a problem or a challenge? Or does the Blamer label you and call you names?

Having a loud inner critic can be a major obstacle to building confidence. This may stem from fears about failing, making mistakes or being criticised, or from worries about being rejected by others.

Your critic can keep you locked in the Comfort Zone and stop you from taking risks that might allow you to grow and develop in life. It may lead to you avoiding difficult situations or putting off starting important challenges. You don't get the chance to test out or act against the unhelpful beliefs of the inner critic. And this just knocks your confidence even further.

Constructive and supportive feedback can help you correct mistakes and find better ways of doing things – moving you from the Comfort Zone to the Stretch or even Growth Zone. But having an overloud or harsh critic can prevent you from hearing and making use of helpful feedback, as you might find it harder to see feedback as an opportunity to learn. If you are always hearing the voice of a loud critic rather than an encouraging inner coach, it may mean you react defensively or angrily when others are trying to help or encourage you to learn.

 Watch This  **4 Minutes**

THE POISONOUS PARROT

 Pause and Think  **2 Minutes**

The Poisonous Parrot
What's your reaction to this video? Make a note here:

....

....

....

Try This  **10 Minutes**

Coping with your inner critic
Do you have a critical inner voice like a Poisonous Parrot that is negative, unhelpful and blocking your confidence? Is it keeping you stuck in the Comfort Zone and making you doubt your abilities?

We all have negative thoughts from time to time, but there are ways to conquer self-doubt. Here are some ideas for how you might respond differently when your Poisonous Parrot starts squawking its negative and self-critical stories.

What to try	How will you use this? What could you try?
Throw a cloth over the cage: Let the parrot squawk but don't let its negative stories stop you from trying something important – just go for it!	
Listen to your Wise Mind: Take a balanced view in which you are able to accept some of the helpful suggestions for improvement but ignore any unfair or unhelpful criticisms that your mind throws up.	
Talk to others: Find someone supportive and caring, and share some of your difficulties. Ask them how they got past their own life challenges and coped when things were tough or scary.	
Pause and notice: Observe when you start talking down your skills and losing confidence. Use this as a signal to pause and check in with yourself. Sometimes, feeling a bit uncomfortable means that something important or exciting is coming up. Take a breath and focus on your next helpful step to get past this tricky situation.	
Write it down: When your mind is being negative or downbeat, try jotting down your thoughts in a notebook, on a laptop or on your phone. Getting the thoughts out of your head may help create some perspective and find new ways to look at the situation.	

Take a reality check: Are things really as bad as you are thinking? Are you jumping to conclusions or exaggerating problems whilst ignoring all the things that are going well? Look at the big picture rather than getting stuck on just a few negatives.

Remember your strengths: When in doubt, go back to your list of personal qualities. These skills, talents and abilities don't just disappear as soon as something goes wrong, and they can act as an important reminder of what you are truly capable of.

Head towards your goal: Finally, ask yourself whether thinking this way is likely to help you achieve your goals? If not, try focusing on what you might do to solve the problem, or think about what you can learn from the situation to help you in future.

Make a plan: Which of the steps above will you try next time your confidence is shaky and your self-critic is giving you a hard time?

Read This   5 Minutes

BRINGING IT TOGETHER: GROW SKILLS IN ACTION

Eli has only basic cooking skills because her mum or older brother usually pre-pare most meals. She feels confident to make breakfast and snacks, but she is not confident to do the shopping and cook full meals. She's never done this before and isn't sure how to use the oven properly, budget for meals or buy the right quantities... So many aspects to keeping herself well fed!

Eli is now leaving home to go to college and feels nervous. She notices herself listening to her inner critic, who starts telling Eli what a useless cook she is and how she will look stupid in front of her new housemates. These thoughts spiral into a general rant to herself about how she should be more capable in many ways.

Then Eli starts to use her GROW skills. She reminds herself that going to college is what she has always dreamed of and she wants to get the best out of the experience. She decides that rather than putting things off and worrying, she will break the problem down into small steps and take action.

Instead of labelling herself as a 'useless cook' and giving up, she takes three slow breaths and focuses on the colours and sounds around. This helps her to stop picturing herself failing to cook at college and being ridiculed. She changes the voice of the critic she hears in her head into a squawking, bird-brained parrot and decides she is not going to listen and let it affect her.

She takes one step out of her Comfort Zone and makes a plan of action. She decides to practise cooking a meal with a supportive close friend who will be encouraging if her first attempt is not perfect. She asks for some help from her mum one evening and buys a recipe book. At home, she practises cooking a roast dinner alongside her brother, who has done this many times before.

Finally, she cooks a full roast dinner for her friend, who tells her it tastes great. Eli accepts the compliment gracefully, allowing herself to feel good about it, even if it was not perfect and the roast potatoes were a bit burnt — it is a work in progress! Next week, spaghetti bolognaise...

What we have covered in Chapter 8: Creating Confidence to Be You

→ Having confidence involves believing in yourself and your abilities, Following your Guide and allowing the 'real' you to be seen by others.

→ You can choose to take confidence-boosting actions, even if you feel anxious or have some inner doubts, as you step outside the safety of your Comfort Zone and into the Stretch and Growth Zones.

→ Observe and Open skills can help you build confidence, to pause and recognise your choices and to cope with uncomfortable thoughts and feelings as you start taking risks and trying new things.

→ Building confidence involves learning and adapting to the challenges you are facing, bouncing back from setbacks and obstacles and building on the changes you make with practice.

→ Motivating yourself with kindness and not pushing yourself too far or too fast will improve your confidence and your performance and help keep you out of the Overload Zone.

→ Building a Confident Mindset involves focusing on your next step, having a 'can-do' attitude and cutting down on negatively comparing yourself with others.

→ You don't have to listen to a loud self-critic or take their negative messages too seriously. Instead, try to recognise your own skills, strengths and personal qualities and allow yourself to accept and absorb positive feedback and praise.

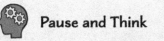 **Pause and Think**  **5 Minutes**

→ What are the most important messages for you from this chapter?

→ What have you learned or understood after reading it and trying the exercises?

....

....

....

Taking action

→ What are you going to do differently now?

→ What actions will you take as a result of reading this chapter?

→ What will you practise on a regular basis in order to build on what you have learned?

....

....

....

Chapter 9

BUILDING FRIENDSHIPS AND CONFIDENT COMMUNICATION

→ Do you feel isolated or lonely, and long to feel more connected to friends or family?

→ Do you ever avoid activities because you are worried about appearing foolish or stupid in front of others?

→ Are you confident to stand up for yourself and say how you feel, and do you know how to resolve conflicts with other people?

→ Want to use the GROW steps to improve your relationships and communication? Read on...

 **Read This** 🕐 **10 Minutes**

The importance of friendships

Strong connections with other people are essential for humans to survive and thrive. They provide a sense of belonging, offer support when life is tough and increase happiness and emotional wellbeing. Yet, a growing number of young people report feeling isolated, lonely and disconnected from other people.

Feeling lonely or isolated is not necessarily about how many people you know or spend time with. You can be happy spending time alone, enjoying your own company, or feel lonely whilst surrounded by people in a crowded room. It's helpful to have a variety of connections, with some friends to chat about superficial things, like the latest sports game, or sharing a funny video, and a smaller number of close relationships where you can share your deeper feelings and the things that really matter to you.

We live in an age of social media, where much of our communication and socialising takes place online. This brings many benefits, and for some people it can encourage friendships and social interaction. But for others, it can become a substitute for real connection. Spending too much time online or gaming can reduce your face-to-face interactions and change the quality of your relationships. And social media posts can be open to misinterpretations and lead to unhelpful comparisons and fear of missing out.

As you move towards adulthood and independence, becoming the unique person you wish to be, you might find that you have less in common or there may be conflict with your parents and family. As a result, you may find yourself seeking increased connection with friends and peers and become disconnected from your family or feel more isolated at home.

Finding a balance is helpful: this means strengthening relationships within your family, finding ways to reconnect if there is strain or disagreement at home, whilst remaining true to your own values, and also finding ways to develop your independence and grow and strengthen friendships and connections with peers. You can use this chapter to find ways to improve the way you relate to all the different people in your life.

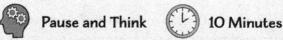 **Pause and Think** **10 Minutes**

Are you feeling lonely, isolated or disconnected?

Feeling lonely or isolated from time to time is common and may be nothing to worry about. But spending a lot of time alone can lead to stress, anxiety and low mood, and can affect your confidence. If you are noticing that feelings of loneliness are growing stronger or are more frequent, it may be helpful to work on strengthening your social connections.

Answer the following questions to help you decide whether you are feeling lonely:

Common signs of loneliness	Do you notice this often? Yes/No
I feel like I have no one to talk to.	
I don't feel that anyone understands me.	
I would like to spend more time with others.	
I feel left out, alone or excluded.	
It is hard to reach out to or communicate with people around me.	

No one really knows me well.
It is difficult for me to make friends.
I cope with feeling uncomfortable around people by eating, drinking alcohol, taking drugs or smoking.
I compare myself unfavourably with others.
I feel angry towards people who don't understand me.
I strongly defend myself when I feel criticised or rejected.
I push people away or make fun of them when they try to get closer to me.

 **Read This** 🕐 **5 Minutes**

Friendship circles

There are lots of things you can do to help tackle feelings of loneliness. Developing friendships takes time and effort, but the pay-off may be to feel happier, better able to cope with stress and problems, and more supported and encouraged to do the things that are important to you.

To start with, let's use friendship circles to look at the different groups of relationships that you have in your life.

→ **Family**: Your closest relationships are usually those at home; this may include both humans and pets.

→ **Close friends and relatives**: These refer to strong friendships with people you can trust and confide in and who would support you in difficult times.

→ **Mates**: People who you hang out with or see regularly.

→ **Distant friends and acquaintances**: People you don't know well or you just know on sight.

→ **Strangers**: People you don't yet know.

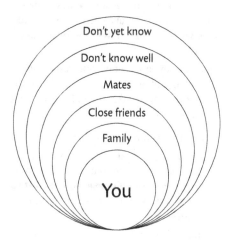

Pause and Think 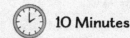 **10 Minutes**

Ready for Action: GROW your existing friendships and relationships

Look at your own friendship and relationship circles. Is there anyone that you haven't connected with for a while or someone in the outer circles that you'd like to become closer to? Choose one or more people and make a note of any names below:

....

....

....

Now look at the following tips and pick which ideas you would like to try.

Tips for improving close relationships	How could this help? Can you try this? Who with?
Find something you both enjoy Think about an activity that you both have in common and are likely to enjoy. Example: Invite a friend to play tennis or football in the park, or to play an online game together.	
Show you are interested Think about the last time someone showed genuine interest in you and what you had to say. How did it make you feel? What did they say or do that showed interest? Can you try this? Example: Invite someone who you know is struggling and needs support for a 'walk and talk' at the park. Make sure to listen to what is bothering them.	
Make time and minimise distractions Think about places and situations that make it easier to talk or give your full attention to someone. Put your phone in your pocket to stop yourself constantly checking it during the conversation. Example: Ask your brother or sister how their day went during mealtimes or a car journey.	

Share your interests and your best qualities

Remember the qualities you have that other people appreciate, such as loyalty, trust, genuineness and good humour.

Example: Choose a friend with a similar interest and ask if they need your help with something they care about, such as studying for a test or training for a sports challenge.

Laughter is the best medicine

Sharing laughter and humour is a great way to connect with others. What do you both find funny or enjoyable? Is there a way to do more of this?

Example: Share a funny video with friends on social media or invite a friend to watch a comedy on TV with you.

Reconnect with friends or family

Have you lost contact with a close friend or are you feeling disconnected from someone in your family? What small steps could you take to reconnect?

Example: Join (or re-join) a drama group or sports team to catch up with old friends. Offer to watch a TV programme or share a cup of tea with a family member who you'd like to feel closer to again.

Add your own ideas

What else can you think of that might deepen your connection to close friends and family?

 Read This   3 Minutes

Widening friendship circles

The next step is to find ways to widen your net and increase your friendship circles. We all seek different things from friendships. Some people like to have deep, profound conversations, while others prefer to keep things light and humorous. Many people develop friendships through shared activities and interests or shared values and passions. So, it is important to recognise what is important to you in a friendship.

It's also helpful to stay flexible and not place too many expectations or demands on any of your friends. Aim to have a range of friends who you can connect with at different times and for your varied interests and needs. For example, you might have friends who you share a love of music with, others that you do exercise with and still others that you feel comfortable talking to about your feelings and ideas. It's not necessary for one person to meet all these needs – this can put too much pressure on a friendship.

 **Try This** ⏰ **10 Minutes**

Using your Guide to widen friendship circles

Think about what different interests and needs you have that might be shared with friends. Place a tick next to any of the areas that are relevant to your life and start to make plans for how you might share these with friends.

Life area	Is this important or relevant at the moment? Yes/No	List possible activities and steps towards connecting with people through this value. Keep the steps small and achievable!
Talking and sharing your feelings and ideas		
Sport, physical activity, and exercise		
Education and learning		
Music (listening and playing)		
Performing and public speaking		
Work, volunteering, contributing		
Computers, online gaming and social media		

Being creative and making things	
Fixing or repairing things	
Staying healthy and caring for your body	
Spiritual and religious values	
What else are you interested in? List your ideas here:	

 **Read This** **5 Minutes**

Creating new friendships

Creating new friendships takes time – a stranger can't grow into a close friend overnight! Try not to put pressure on yourself to make friends immediately. Instead, focus on spending more time around people with shared interests by joining in activities that involve others. This may also give you a sense of purpose and help you discover new interests or talents!

The first steps to making new friendships can be very small and achievable. Perhaps a stranger becomes someone that you don't know well or just know on sight. In time, they may grow to become a mate, and eventually even a close friend, but this process will happen naturally and there's no rush.

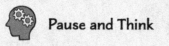 Pause and Think 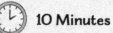 10 Minutes

Making new friends

In this activity, we will look at some tips for moving people up the friendship ladder from the outer circles to just a little closer to you.

Tip for making new friends	Can you try this? When? Where?
Notice who is around you Try not to get so caught up in your mind that you don't notice the people around you. You might miss a friendly expression from a potential new friend! Just brief eye contact and a small smile can be the first step up the friendship ladder.	
Involve yourself in a group activity Joining a club or group or attending an event will enable you to meet like-minded people with shared interests. What could you try? It could be anything from a book club, sport, drama group, quiz team, chess club – the list is endless!	
Arrive early This will give you the chance to introduce yourself while there are only a few people there, chat informally and get to know people.	
Ask someone a question If you are feeling unsure about what to say, asking a question is a great way to start a conversation. Choose someone with a friendly expression and ask how their day is going. This may feel scary at first, but taking one small brave step can create a tiny connection, which might just grow into a deeper friendship.	

What else could you try? List your ideas here:

 **Read This**  **5 Minutes**

Friendship-blocking habits

Some patterns of thinking or behaving can act as 'friendship blockers', which can get in the way of building the friendships that you really want.

Tanya is worried that people will think she is boring. When sitting at lunch, the group start chatting about their plans for the weekend. Tanya immediately gets out her phone and starts scrolling through and avoids eye contact with everyone. Then she makes an excuse and rushes off to the toilet so that no one will be able to judge her for being boring.

Because of her avoidance actions, which included leaving the group, Tanya misses out on an invitation to a party on Saturday evening. She feels too shy to ask to go when she later hears other people talking about it and ends up feeling even more isolated and lonely.

What connection-blocking habits is Tanya using in this situation? What else could she try?

 **Pause and Think** 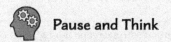 **10 Minutes**

Thoughts that block friendships

Many different fears and worries might pop up in your mind as you start thinking about trying to widen your social network.

As you imagine trying a new activity with an unknown group of people, your mind might start predicting all kinds of terrible scenarios.

I'll have nothing to say and everyone will think I'm boring.

I'll say something weird and everyone will laugh at me.

Or some Unwanted Mind Visitors might pay a visit.

The Name-Caller:
You look such a fool
What an idiot you are!

The Scaremonger:
No one will talk to you and you'll
be standing on your own!

Look through the list of common thoughts that get in the way of connecting with others below and see if you recognise any of these.

Friendship-blocking thoughts	Do you recognise this? Yes/No
Self-critical thoughts about being boring, weird or not good enough.	
Catastrophic thoughts about all the things that might go wrong if you try to make new friends.	
Memories from past experiences when you felt embarrassed or rejected by others.	
Ignoring or discounting all the times that things have gone well for you in the past.	
Imagining other people looking disapproving or laughing at you.	
Memories or images of yourself looking stupid or awkward in front of others.	
Worrying that you will be the centre of attention with everyone staring at you.	

Now think about this: What impact do these thoughts have on you? How do they change your behaviour and your willingness to try to connect with others?

How might it alter your feelings or actions if you learned to ignore these thoughts and images? What effect could this have on you and your relationships with others?

Coping with negative thoughts

These thoughts and images are not facts – they are opinions and guesses about what might happen, which may or may not be true. And you don't have to believe the thoughts if they are unhelpful or getting in the way of enjoying your life.

The more attention you give to negative thoughts, the more anxious you are likely to feel. You are more likely to avoid interactions with others and do things that keep potential friends at a distance. This keeps you stuck in a negative spiral.

Can you recognise any Unwanted Mind Visitors from Chapter 4 that are coming in and spoiling your fun and enjoyment? Is the Pessimist or the Blamer hanging around in your head? Think of ways you can spot them but not pay attention to their unhelpful chatter.

In Chapter 8 on building confidence, we talked about taking 'confident actions', even if you are experiencing worry, doubts or uncertainty. This involves behaving 'as if' you feel a little more confident and might involve choosing to take small steps towards opening up to people, even if negative thoughts show up. This will help to build your confidence and improve your relationships with others.

 **Read This** 10 Minutes

Where is your attention?

When feeling anxious in a social situation, it is common to turn your attention inwards, putting what you do, what you say and how you look in the spotlight. You might be focusing your attention in one of these ways.

- → **Becoming hyper-aware of your body** and any physical sensations of anxiety such as a racing heart, sweaty palms or how much you are blushing.

- → **Getting caught up in negative stories** and thoughts about your performance.

- → **Focusing too much on how you appear to others**, including over-planning what to say next and constantly checking your appearance.

- → **Repeatedly checking for threats or problems**, such as whether anyone is laughing at you or criticising you.

- → **Jumping to negative conclusions**, so when you notice someone frown, yawn or glance at their watch, you assume it means they are finding you boring rather than that they are tired.

 **Read This** 5 Minutes

Take the focus off yourself

Self-focus can be a friendship-blocking action that makes it harder to cope in social situations. Self-focus means turning your attention inwards and getting preoccupied with what's happening in your body or what you are saying. This makes it harder to listen to others or get involved fully with the people around you. You are also more likely to pick up on any subtle sensations of anxiety in your body and might exaggerate or jump to negative conclusions about how anxious you appear, because your attention is focused inwards.

Try This   5 Minutes

Use listening skills to bring your focus outside yourself

Next time you are feeling anxious in a social situation, bring your awareness **outside** your body to whatever you are doing. Use your five senses, including listening extra closely to what the other person is saying. Allow your natural curiosity and interest to guide you. Take the pressure off: you don't need to say anything straight away, but if there is a pause, you could try asking an open question such as, 'Can you tell me about...?', which will encourage the other person to continue talking. Remember to give the other person your full attention and let conversation flow naturally.

Read This   5 Minutes

Friendship-blocking and friendship-enabling actions

Trying to avoid social situations that might make you feel anxious or distressed can become a friendship-blocking action that stops you getting the chance to build friendships and will often knock your confidence and increase your anxiety in the long run.

To develop friendships, we need to give out signals to others that we are friendly and willing to connect. Friendship-blocking actions might also involve behaviours such as avoiding eye contact, keeping your head down to stop people seeing you blush or repeatedly rehearsing what you plan to say in advance. You might even go as far as deliberately pushing people away or making cutting remarks to avoid the hurt of potential rejection or anxiety. Again, these actions tend to do more harm than good. Rather than hiding anxiety, they often draw more attention to it and may worsen the anxiety spiral.

Read This   5 Minutes

Cole arrives at a small gathering of people at a friend's house. When he enters the kitchen, he sees a small group of people chatting and laughing. Cole immediately feels anxious and has a flurry of negative thoughts such as, 'I'll make a fool of myself and start blushing and sweating if I try to talk to them!' He imagines the whole group staring and laughing at him as he stumbles through his words.

Cole walks over to the group, but it is hard to focus on what they are saying because he's feeling so anxious. All he can think about is how noticeable his blushing and sweating must be.

He keeps his gaze down on the ground to try to keep the others from noticing his flushed cheeks and holds his arms close to his sides in case he has sweat marks on his shirt. This makes it hard to hold his drink.

Cole tries desperately to think what he can say that might be interesting to the others. But he is so busy being self-focused and trying to appear calm that he's not listening to what the others are talking about, and it feels impossible to join in the conversation.

After a short while, Cole makes his excuses and goes home, feeling fed up and sad.

Pause and Think   5 Minutes

→ What friendship-blocking actions did Cole choose?

→ What else could Cole try if he is feeling anxious in this situation? Which direction is his Guide likely to be pointing? What small steps could he take that might move his life in this direction and reduce his feelings of isolation and loneliness?

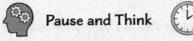

Pause and Think   10 Minutes

Do you notice any of the following friendship-blocking habits in yourself?

Friendship-blocking habit	Do you notice this? Yes/No
Spending a lot of time alone watching TV or playing computer games.	
Keeping your head down and avoiding eye contact.	
Using text instead of phoning.	
Spending a lot of time on social media.	

cont.

Friendship-blocking habit	Do you notice this? Yes/No
Playing on your mobile phone when sitting with others.	
Staying plugged in to your headphones when you are out and about.	
Taking lunchbreaks alone or working through breaks.	
Not finding time to respond to friends' emails or messages.	
Running your whole life online and not making time to see anyone face to face.	
What other friendship-blocking habits can you notice? Write these down here:	

 **Pause and Think**   **5 Minutes**

How many of these habits do you recognise in yourself? How much of an effect might they be having on your friendships and connections with others? What could you do instead that would encourage and nurture friendships? **Move on to the next exercise for some ideas.**

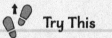 **Try This**   **10 Minutes**

Friendship-enabling actions

Friendship-enabling action	When and where will you try this?
Smile and say hello to someone when you enter a room.	
Pay extra attention when someone is talking.	
Start up a conversation with someone.	

Keep your phone in your pocket when eating dinner with your family.	
Respond to a friend's message or send one to someone you've not heard from in a while.	
Take off your headphones when people are around.	
Phone someone instead of just sending a short message.	
Take a break from your gaming to go to the park and kick a football.	
Go and sit with someone at lunch instead of hiding behind a computer or phone.	
What are your ideas? Add these below...	

Read This **5 Minutes**

Healthy and unhealthy friendships

Healthy friendships will boost your confidence, help you feel more connected and support you through difficult times. In a healthy friendship, you enjoy spending time together, treat one another as equals and appreciate each other's differences. A healthy friend will respect your decisions and opinions, and will be honest and trustworthy, keeping things you share with them in confidence, without spreading gossip or rumours. You celebrate each other's successes and stand up for each other in the face of bullies or problems.

Healthy friendships are mostly kind and supportive, but there will sometimes be disagreements or differences of opinion, and even a healthy friend may sometimes act out of character or hurt your feelings. But a healthy friend will take responsibility for their actions and apologise if they do make a mistake like slipping up and sharing something private.

It's also important to look out for patterns of negative behaviour that might suggest a friendship is unhealthy or even involves bullying. Unhealthy friendships can trigger anxiety and knock your confidence and self-esteem, and may involve someone who:

→ tries to control or manipulate you, or places unreasonable demands on you

→ makes fun of you or calls you names

→ talks down or is rude to you, saying your opinions are stupid or don't make sense

→ spreads rumours or gossip about you

→ makes hurtful jokes at your expense but accuses you of being too sensitive

→ makes you feel uncomfortable or embarrasses you

→ makes you feel alone or different, or targets you because of your sexuality, religion, race, gender or disability.

It can sometimes be hard to decide if difficulties with a friend are crossing the boundary or whether you might be misinterpreting their attempt at humour or simply have a different point of view, but the rule of thumb remains: if it hurts (physically or emotionally) – then don't tolerate it! Discrimination and bullying is not acceptable anywhere in our society or our world.

Here are some of our tips for GROWing healthy friendships.

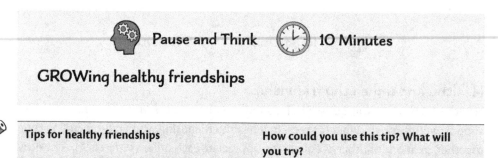

Pause and Think   10 Minutes

GROWing healthy friendships

Tips for healthy friendships	How could you use this tip? What will you try?
Follow your Guide towards healthy friendships Think about how you wish to be as a friend and how you would like others to see you and treat you. Follow your Guide in making decisions about which friendships are truly worth your time and energy and about how you wish to treat others.	

Be your own champion

Can you be a healthy friend to yourself by standing up to rather than being pushed around by others or even your own thoughts? What steps can you take to look out for yourself? What advice would your inner champion or coach give? Sharing your feelings with a trusted friend or adult may also help. The next section, 'Confident Caring Communication', gives tips on what to say if you need to express yourself.

Take action and control what you can

Sometimes, just ignoring negative comments and not rising to the bait may be all you need to try. You can also make active choices to look after yourself, such as putting a block on someone's email address or staying in places where you have support from healthy friends and adults.

Kindness is a superpower

Being kind to yourself and others can bring strength and resilience in tough times, helping you and others to cope. Remember, whatever you are facing, you are not alone. Can you wish well to all the many people who are struggling with feeling isolated, feeling lonely and worrying about what others think, or have problems with bullying and difficulties within friendships, and include yourself amongst this group?

Support yourself and others

What small steps can you take to reach out to someone else who might be struggling with loneliness or isolation? Maybe it's making someone feel more included, or maybe it's not staying silent when you notice hurtful actions or words around you. Is there someone you could reach out to for support for yourself?

Imagine yourself coping

Can you imagine yourself coping in a challenging situation? If you fear tripping over and being teased as you enter a party, see yourself getting up again, brushing yourself down, laughing it off and continuing to join in, despite the urge to flee. What other resources could you draw on in this situation? Can you plan what to say or how to deal with criticism or hurtful banter? Planning ways to cope with problems can build your confidence to give scary situations a try.

 **Read This** (🕐) **5 Minutes**

Confident Caring Communication

Communication is the building block of life and influences how you relate to yourself and to other people. Being able to communicate effectively is an important skill that humans have developed to enable us to function in social groups. Improving your communication skills can help you to build positive relationships with people in your life and develop your confidence and self-esteem.

But communicating with others is not always straightforward or easy and can sometimes involve conflicts and misunderstanding, leading to feelings of frustration, sadness and isolation.

Confident Caring Communication (CCC) is a way of talking to ourselves and others with understanding and respect. It can improve relationships, help resolve conflict and help you to recognise and meet your personal needs. Some of the important skills of CCC include being able to:

→ express your ideas, opinions and feelings in an open, direct and honest way

→ stand up for your own rights while respecting the rights of others

→ take responsibility for yourself and your actions without judging or blaming other people

→ find ways to connect, cooperate and compromise when dealing with disagreements or conflict.

CCC is based on three important principles.

→ **All human beings are equal** and have the right to be respected, heard and understood. Effective communication is not about convincing others to do what you want but expressing your thoughts and feelings with honesty and being willing to hear other people's point of view. The aim is to find a fair way to move forwards that meets everyone's needs.

→ **We are all part of common humanity**: Focusing on what you have in common with the other person rather than your differences encourages understanding and mutual respect and reduces conflict.

→ **Empathy and compassion**: Empathy involves recognising what is important to you in a particular situation and trying to understand what the other person cares about. Compassion involves being more understanding and accepting and responding with kindness rather than harsh criticism or judgement.

 **Read This**  **5 Minutes**

Four steps to Confident Caring Communication

CCC can be broken down into four simple steps using the acronym DEAR.

1. **D**escribe the situation without judgements or blame.

2. **E**motions: Recognise and express how you are feeling.

3. **A**sk yourself what matters most (to you and to the other person).

4. **R**easonable Request: What can you ask for that might help meet your needs?

Step 1: Describe the situation without judgements or blame

Everyday communication often expresses your **interpretation** and **opinions** about a situation and often includes analysing, judging or criticising other people. This can trigger disagreement and lead to disconnection between the people involved.

An alternative is to simply **describe** the situation without judgement. Some useful tips for this include considering the following questions.

→ Can you describe what happened?

→ What did you see or hear?

→ Can you avoid judgements or blame and still express yourself clearly and honestly? This can be very challenging at times!

Our aim in CCC is to recognise when you are slipping into judgements and criticisms and learn to step back, using your **Open and Observe** skills from Chapter 3, to describe the situation more clearly.

Some of the common traps that we tend to get caught in and that get in the way of CCC are summarised in the chart below.

Pitfalls to avoid	What not to say	What could you say instead?
Making judgements	You should... You never...	I noticed that... It's uncomfortable when I see... I'm hoping for...
Blaming (yourself or others)	If you/I hadn't been so careless... It's your/my fault...	I feel disappointed because... I'm wishing that...
Advising, correcting or explaining	I think you should... Your problem is that...	This seems difficult for you... I'm worried that this happened...

cont.

Pitfalls to avoid	What not to say	What could you say instead?
Storytelling and 'one-upping'	Let me tell you about the time that... You think that's bad! I've been through much worse...	I'm remembering some similar experiences, but I'd like to hear your thoughts first...
Making demands	I need you to... You have to... I want...	What's important to me is... I've got some thoughts about what I'd like us do and I'm also willing to listen to your ideas...
Name calling and criticism	You're such an idiot... Can't you just follow simple instructions?	I can see that something has gone wrong... It looks like an important step was missed out...

 Pause and Think **10 Minutes**

Look at these examples of different ways of talking about a difficult situation. For the first few examples, we have included some judgements and then made a suggested alternative that involves describing and observing. Can you complete the final few examples yourself? Be as creative as you like and feel free to adapt the situation to make it more relevant to your own life and experiences.

Using judgement, blaming or criticising	Describing the situation
It was a terrible morning and my day was ruined by the appalling traffic!	There was a lot of traffic this morning, which made me late for an important appointment.
You are so snappy and rude when you get home from work.	You spoke in short, sharp sentences with an angry tone of voice when I asked how your day was.
You're an irresponsible liar. You said you had given up smoking, but I saw you sneaking around in the garden last night.	I noticed you smoking in the garden last night.
I'm so useless.	I didn't say anything when the team leader asked what we would prefer to do.
You are so irritating and annoying.	
He is always so lazy.	
The problem is that you're too selfish.	
She is so irresponsible!	

 **Read This** 🕐 **5 Minutes**

Step 2: Emotions: Recognise and express how you are feeling

The next part of learning to communicate using CCC is to recognise and express your feelings and emotions. This is not always easy, especially when the feelings are strong and arise quickly; you can be caught up in them before you realise what's happened. Spotting your feelings involves asking yourself questions such as these.

→ How do I feel about this? What emotions can I notice?

→ What is driving this? What's behind my reaction?

→ What's the worst part of this for me?

Try to give your feelings a name, saying: 'I'm feeling frustrated... hurt... excited... hopeful...' Knowing how you are feeling will help you to understand what's important and can help you to understand what might improve a difficult situation.

I'm worried. I'm feeling hurt. I'm excited. I'm disappointed.

Try to share how you are feeling with the other person, owning your own feelings using 'I' statements. If this makes you uncomfortable, it's fine to leave out the word 'feeling', perhaps saying, 'I'm a bit fed up with this situation' or 'I'm tired and frustrated.'

 **Pause and Think** 🕐 **5 Minutes**

Remind yourself about different feelings

Becoming familiar with your different feelings can help you make sense of what's going on inside and make it easier to express your emotions. To help with this, in Chapter 3, we used a CBT framework to explore a range of different feelings, thoughts, body sensations and actions. Why not flip back to page 61 now and remind yourself?

Choose several situations that you have recently experienced in which communication with another person was difficult in some way. What were your feelings? How do you think the other person may have been feeling?

 **Read This** 🕐 **5 Minutes**

Step 3: Ask yourself what matters most

The next step in CCC is to ask yourself **why** the situation is important to you and to think about what matters to the other person. This is very much like Following your Guide.

To find out what matters, ask yourself these questions.

→ What are your personal values and needs that are important to the current situation?

→ Why is this situation important to you?

→ What could be important to the other person? How might you be feeling if you put yourself in their shoes?

→ Can you imagine what their needs and values might be? How are these different or similar to yours?

Conflicts often arise when people have different opinions about what would be the best strategy to meet a particular need. Identifying each person's need before starting to discuss what to do next encourages connection, builds relationships and creates more space to be creative and brainstorm different ways of dealing with things rather than getting stuck on insisting that there is only one way to solve a complex problem.

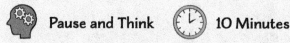 **Pause and Think** 🕐 **10 Minutes**

Here are some of the common human needs. This is not an exhaustive list, and priorities and values differ from person to person. You can add any important needs that affect you in the space below.

→ **Acceptance**: Empathy, love, respect, support.

→ **Achievement**: Being empowered, contribution.

→ **Acknowledgement**: To be valued, appreciated, heard, respected, recognised, to matter.

→ **Autonomy**: Choice about decisions, independence, freedom to be yourself.

→ **Comfort and ease**: Satisfied basic needs: food, water, shelter, air, sleep, rest.

→ **Connection**: Belonging, affection, being included.

→ **Enjoyment**: Fun, play, laughter, excitement, celebration.

→ **Safety and security**: Financial, physical.

→ **Stimulation**: Learning, being creative, using skills.

→ **Trust**: Honesty, equality, fairness.

→ **Any other important needs:**

. . . .

. . . .

. . . .

Look at the list of situations below. For the first few examples, we have made some suggestions about the needs of each person. Complete the chart with your ideas about what needs might be important.

Situation	What might be some of the different needs for each person?
George and Harry are brothers. They are arguing about whose turn it is to do the washing up.	Rest Choice Acknowledgement/being heard
Sally and her mum disagree about what time Sally should come home from a party.	Fun and connection with friends Autonomy Trust Safety
Laura wants to get a part-time job but she's worried about being too busy and not having enough time to study or relax.	Comfort and ease Financial security Autonomy Achievement
What examples can you add from situations you are facing in your life?	

_____

_____

_____

 **Read This**   🕐 **5 Minutes**

Step 4: Reasonable Request

The final step moves on to thinking about what to do next and encourages you to make a Reasonable Request. This might involve asking yourself or the other person to take some action. In this stage, some creative brainstorming will be needed to find a balance between your needs and desires and those of others.

A Reasonable Request only asks for something that the other person has the power to actually do. For example, asking a friend for world peace or a loan of £1 million might be outside most people's control!

A Reasonable Request is also not a demand. This means that the other person has a choice and can say 'no' without being threatened with any kind of punishment if they don't feel able to meet your request.

Here are some examples of Reasonable Requests.

→ Would you be able to talk a bit more quietly?

→ Could you help me understand and explain why you made that choice?

→ Can you tell me how you feel about what happened and what you would like me to do differently next time?

→ Could you pause for 5 minutes to give me time to think about your request?

→ Can you tell me what you heard me say?

Some of these questions may help you to think up a Reasonable Request.

→ What are the most important needs that you identified in Step 3?

→ How might these needs be met? Be as creative as you can. If possible, think of several possible solutions.

→ How can you ask for what you want in a way that's respectful of the other person and likely to be received well?

 **Read This**   🕐 **5 Minutes**

Here is an example of CCC in action.

Plan and prepare	Choose the right time and right place for the conversation. Try not to ambush or surprise the person. Think in advance what you would like from the situation and what you plan to say.	I will go for a walk and chat to my friend as we go along.
Describe the situation	Observe and **describe** the situation or behaviour, without evaluating, judging or blaming.	I noticed that we haven't been spending as much time together lately because you've been so busy with work and your new boyfriend.
Emotions and feelings	Recognise and express how you are feeling – use 'notice and name' to label your emotions. Use 'I' statements to own your feelings.	I feel a bit sad.
Ask yourself what matters most	Think about what needs are most important to you and to the other person. Aim for connection and understanding. Try to show that you have heard what the other person has said and that you understand where they may be coming from.	I really enjoy our friendship and having fun together. We always have such a laugh! I'm guessing you are quite busy, but I hope we can find a way to keep our friendship strong.
Make a Reasonable Request	What would help to meet your important needs in this situation? Be respectful and friendly, and ensure it's not a demand. Look for a strategy that meets everyone's needs and stay flexible until you reach a fair solution.	Would you be happy to put a catch-up date in the diary for a few weeks' time?

 **Try This** 🕐 **10 Minutes**

Now it's your turn! Choose a situation in which you have to communicate a slightly difficult message. Don't pick something that is a big or long-standing problem – start with something that's only a small issue – and plan how you could approach this conversation using CCC.

Plan and prepare	Choose the right time and right place for the conversation. Try not to ambush or surprise the person. Think in advance what you would like from the situation and what you plan to say.	

Describe the situation	Observe and describe the situation or behaviour, without evaluating, judging or blaming.
Emotions and feelings	Recognise and express how you are feeling – use 'notice and name' to label your emotions. Use 'I' statements to own your feelings.
Ask yourself what matters most	Think about what needs are most important to you and to the other person. Aim for connection and understanding. Try to show that you have heard what the other person has said and that you understand where they may be coming from.
Make a Reasonable Request	What would help to meet your important needs in this situation? Be respectful and friendly, and ensure it's not a demand. Look for a strategy that meets everyone's needs and stay flexible until you reach a fair solution.

What we have covered in Chapter 9: Building Friendships and Confident Communication

→ Building healthy friendships and connections with other people can give you a sense of belonging, offer support when life is tough and increase your happiness and emotional wellbeing.

→ You can increase the quality of your friendships by sharing what you care about, listening and accepting others' thoughts and opinions, even if they are different to your own, and looking for ways to laugh and have fun together.

→ Follow your Guide to find ways to expand your friendship circles by involving yourself in group activities so you can share your interests with like-minded others.

→ Instead of allowing friendship-blocking thoughts or actions to get in the way of building friendships, you can step back, follow your inner coach, be kind to yourself and choose Wise actions that take you towards stronger friendships and connections with those that matter to you.

→ Confident Caring Communication can help you to express your opinions and needs with understanding and respect, even when there is conflict or differences of opinion.

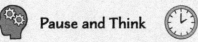 **Pause and Think**  **5 Minutes**

→ What are the most important messages for you from this chapter?

→ What have you learned or understood after reading it and trying the exercises?

....
....
....

Taking action

→ What are you going to do differently after reading this chapter?

→ What actions can you practise or do more of?

→ What is the next step?

....
....
....

Chapter 10

HEALTHY LIFE HABITS

→ Are you having difficulty getting to sleep and finding it even harder to wake up ready to get going in the early mornings?

→ Do you know you should be doing more physical activity to be healthier and happier, but feel stressed because you can't seem to fit it in?

→ Do you ever think it's pointless to bother with a healthy diet now, so you put off starting until later in life?

→ Do you want to ensure you look after yourself now and in the future by building Healthy Life Habits that suit you? Read on...

 **Read This** 🕐 **5 Minutes**

About Healthy Life Habits

There's a lot of information about the importance of a healthy diet, regular exercise and getting good sleep to improve our physical and mental wellbeing. You might even be thinking, 'I've heard all this before... I know what to do already.'

Many people make resolutions to 'get healthy' and start out with great intentions but find it difficult to get started or to keep these changes going. In this chapter, we will think about ways to create Healthy Life Habits – actions that you do automatically and don't even have to think about.

It's sometimes hard to remember that what you do with your body now can have a big impact in the future – especially if that means eating less of the food you like or making sure you get enough sleep or don't party too hard. Who wants to spoil the fun?! But recognising that health is important, both now and for your future happiness, can be the first step to creating Healthy Life Habits.

The key is to know what suits you personally, what's important to you and what keeps you well. Knowing some facts about health might motivate you to take action, encourage you to make Wise choices and inspire you to create a set of habits that you can easily fit in to your life.

It's also important to make yourself a priority. You might need to find a balance and a healthy routine that works for you, without pushing yourself too hard or setting unrealistic expectations for immediate results. This is a life journey! It's about taking one small step in the right direction to start creating your personal healthy life plan.

In this chapter, we will:

➜ summarise some of the key facts about sleep, physical activity and healthy eating

➜ offer some tips to help you create your own healthy life plan and think about ways to overcome obstacles that might get in the way

➜ look at some other Unhealthy Life Habits such as use of technology

➜ use the 10 Minute GROW steps to create Healthy Life Habits.

Jay moved schools just before his GCSEs and was missing his mates who mostly played in the hockey team. He kept in touch on social media, but this took up a lot of time and he found himself comparing his life with those of his former friends, who all seemed to be having fun without him.

Jay's new school focused heavily on rugby, which was not a sport that he enjoyed. He found it more difficult to motivate himself to train and keep up his physical fitness, which had always been important to him before. Jay's new friends were a good laugh, but not sporty, and liked to hang out at the local fast-food restaurant. Jay found himself craving burgers and chips and started eating these more often than he used to. He gained weight and started to lose the toned look in his body that he used to take pride in. He started to feel sluggish and had difficulty concentrating on his schoolwork.

Jay had always been a good sleeper and an early riser but now found that he couldn't get himself out of bed in the morning, as he was gaming into the early hours and having restless nights. His parents were disappointed in Jay's mock results, and his mum kept nagging him about the state of his room and his lack of effort in many areas of his life. Jay felt irritable and fed up.

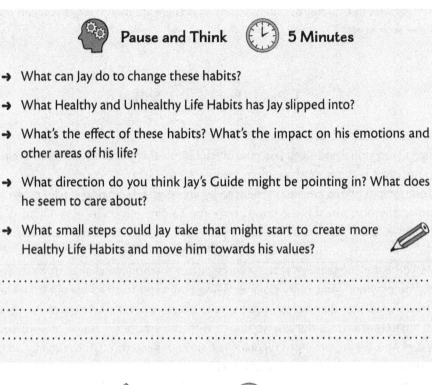

Pause and Think **5 Minutes**

→ What can Jay do to change these habits?

→ What Healthy and Unhealthy Life Habits has Jay slipped into?

→ What's the effect of these habits? What's the impact on his emotions and other areas of his life?

→ What direction do you think Jay's Guide might be pointing in? What does he seem to care about?

→ What small steps could Jay take that might start to create more Healthy Life Habits and move him towards his values?

....

....

....

Read This **5 Minutes**

Do you need better sleep?

We all need sleep! It's essential for rest and recuperation, for growth and development and for emotional and physical wellbeing. Not getting enough sleep can have many damaging effects on young people, including weight gain, low mood and depression, poor performance and concentration, reduced creativity and lower immunity to diseases.

The causes of sleep trouble

It's common to have trouble sleeping, and many things can interfere with a good night's sleep. It's often hard to sleep during important life events, even positive ones, such as parties or holidays. Sleep problems can also be triggered by life stresses and worries about exams, homework, relationships, social activities and jobs, which all make it difficult to relax and fall asleep at night.

Could your technology habits be interfering with your sleep? If you are finding it hard to switch off from technology at night, and playing games, messaging friends or watching videos, you might find it harder to get good quality sleep. We talk more about this later in the chapter. The good news is there are many things you can do to improve your sleep.

Read This   **5 Minutes**

How much sleep do you need?

We are all individual and sleep patterns differ, but on the whole, eight to ten hours of sleep per night is about right for young people aged 11–24.

Your sleep patterns are also influenced by an internal biological clock known as a 'circadian rhythm', which is the body's response to different levels of sunlight. When it's bright outside, you feel more alert and awake. When it becomes dark, the body produces hormones such as melatonin, which makes you feel sleepy.

As you enter the teenage years, your circadian rhythm can change quite dramatically. You may find your body clock is telling you to go to sleep several hours later and to wake up later than before. You become a night owl rather than a morning lark. Unfortunately, this does not always match with the school timetable or your social calendar! And, it's important to regularly get enough sleep through the week and not to try to 'catch up' missed sleep at weekends.

The **quality** of your sleep is also important. Our brains and bodies need a certain number of hours of deep sleep to revitalise, function at our best, learn and grow. Stress, worry and low mood can affect sleep quality, as well as stimulants such as caffeine, alcohol and drugs. Alcohol and certain drugs can become a 'false friend' – making you relaxed and sleepy at bedtime but then causing you to wake early or have disturbed sleep that is less refreshing.

Read This   **5 Minutes**

Screens and sleep

Devices such as smartphones, tablets, computers and TV screens give off short-wavelength blue light that is very similar to sunlight. This light makes you more alert and can trick the body into thinking that it's still daytime. So, using these devices late at night or before bed can interfere with your sleep.

SLEEP TIPS AND SCREEN USE

→ Cut down late-night use of electronic devices, especially those that are held close to your face, such as phones and tablets.

→ Dim the screen or use a night mode with warmer tones in the evening.

→ Can you keep your bedroom as a 'screen-free zone'? If this is not an option, try turning all devices off at least an hour before bedtime.

→ Charge your phone in another room overnight so that incoming messages and notifications don't affect your sleep.

What small actions or steps can you commit to for your use of electronic devices or screens that might help with your sleep?

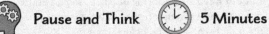

Do you need to take action about your sleep?

The occasional poor night of sleep is completely normal and will not cause any long-term harm. But if you've been sleeping badly for a few weeks or longer, this may be a good time to make a change. The first step is to keep track of your sleep amount and quality over one or two weeks.

Day/Date	What time did you go to sleep?	What time did you wake up?	Rate the quality of your sleep: How rested or energetic did you feel afterwards? (1–10)	Notes: Things that might have affected your sleep (helpful or unhelpful) or any disturbance to your routine.

 **Try This** **10 Minutes**

Tips for improving your sleep

I have trouble getting to sleep	**Set a regular sleep pattern**: Stick to similar times for going to bed and waking up no matter what you are doing, and avoid sleeping in too long after a poor night's sleep or a party.
	Create a 'wind-down' routine: This prepares your body and mind for sleep. Plan a relaxing activity that doesn't involve an electronic screen, such as reading, listening to an audiobook, having a bath or doing yoga.
	Avoid late-night technology: Bright screens late at night can disrupt the sleep–wake cycle.
	Make a 'sleep haven': Ensure your bedroom is dark during sleep hours, quiet and not too cluttered and that your bed is comfortable and the room is a good temperature for sleeping.
	Cut out daytime naps: The odd nap after an unusually late night is fine, but don't let this become a regular habit. If you really need to nap, make it short (15 minutes or less) and before 3 pm.
	Reduce caffeine, nicotine, alcohol or other stimulants, especially within six hours of bedtime. Remember, a lot of fizzy drinks also contain caffeine. Avoid heavy meals late at night.
	Cover the clock: Checking the time can lead to worry and impatience. Set the alarm and then wait until morning.
I have trouble staying asleep, or I wake early. My sleep pattern is all over the place.	**Sleep when you feel sleepy**: Only try to sleep when you feel tired rather than spending hours lying awake in bed.
	Get up and try again later: If you can't get to sleep after about 20 minutes, get out of bed and do something calming or boring, like sitting in a dimly lit room. When you feel sleepy, return to bed and try to sleep again. Repeat the process if you still can't sleep.
	Only use your bed for sleep and rest: If you do homework in your room, have a separate desk or work area. Keep electronic devices such as phones, computers and TVs out of the bedroom.
I have trouble waking up, or I wake up exhausted.	**Avoid long lie-ins**: Too much rest can make you more tired, particularly if it is linked to low mood.
	Keep to your usual routine: Get up even if you are tired. Try putting your alarm clock on the other side of the room or taking a refreshing shower to liven you up.
	Make your bed as soon as you get up, so you are not tempted to crawl back in.
	Regular daytime physical activity keeps your body healthy and often helps more with fatigue than focusing on sleeping.

I have worries or sad thoughts, dreams or memories that keep me awake or wake me up.	**Low mood or anxiety can affect sleep**: Look at the chapters in this book for some helpful ideas and share your concerns with a trusted adult who can offer support. **Write down problems or worries** in a journal or notebook. Do this well before bedtime and plan how you could cope with any difficulties. Use 'Thinking Time' if you are kept awake by an active mind (see Chapter 7 on Anxiety). **Don't try too hard**: You can't force yourself to sleep! Worrying about sleep will make you more anxious and keep you awake longer. Getting up for a short while might help. Remember, even a small amount of sleep is valuable. **You can cope better than you think**: A night without sleep is not a disaster. Think about ways of coping and taking care of yourself, and find ways of reducing demands the next day.

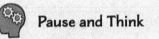 **Pause and Think** 🕐 **5 Minutes**

Next steps for healthy sleep...

Now that you have learned the importance of healthy sleep habits, what are your next steps? What small actions or steps can you plan that might help improve your sleep routine? This could be anything from increasing your day-time physical activity to planning a nightly wind-down routine where you put your phone out of sight and enjoy relaxing in a warm bath at bedtime!

What will you try? Make a note of your thoughts here:

....

....

....

📖 **Read This** 🕐 **5 Minutes**

Physical activity and movement

The benefits of keeping active can't be exaggerated. If a doctor could use a prescription pad to write down things you could do to keep healthy, physical activity would be top of the list! It can have major benefits for your emotional and physical health and wellbeing.

Physical activity doesn't just mean exercise. It involves anything that gets you up and moving your body, including walking, climbing stairs, house chores, getting out with the dog, even standing up, stretching and walking around your computer desk. All of these things can help you to be more active.

Experts are also increasingly aware of the damaging impact of being **inactive**. Many activities such as watching TV, reading, sitting at a computer or travelling in a car all involve staying still for long periods. These are important parts of modern life, but we need to balance them with other activities where we are active and moving.

What are the benefits of physical activity?

There are many benefits of being more physically active. Take a look at the chart below and make a note of which of these reasons are most important to you.

Benefit	Examples	How is this important to you personally?
Improves physical health	Improves your heart and lung health. Boosts your immune system. Helps develop strong muscles and bones and good posture. Reduces body fat and helps keep a healthy body weight. Reduces risk of heart problems, high blood pressure, cancer and diabetes.	
Improves mood and reduces stress	More energy and vitality. Greater enjoyment and happiness. Reduced stress, anxiety, anger and depression. Improved sleep.	
Provides social contact and support	A great way to develop friendships and connect with others. Creates meaning and purpose.	
Improves concentration and focus	Improves concentration, memory, focus and thinking skills. Can be used to break up long periods of sitting or studying.	
Develops self-confidence	A way of learning new skills and building self-confidence and self-esteem.	

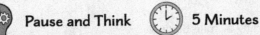 **Pause and Think** 🕐 **5 Minutes**

How much activity is healthy?

It is recommended that young people carry out around 60 minutes per day of moderate to vigorous physical activity. This should include a combination of aerobic exercise and exercises to strengthen your muscles and bones. It's also important to minimise the amount of time spent sitting or not moving.

Does this recommendation sound like a lot? Or does it sound about right? If you spend a lot of time doing, and are very committed to, sport and activity, this may not sound like enough!

We are all different, and what is realistic and achievable for some may seem impossible for others.

Make a note of your thoughts here:

....

....

....

📖 **Read This** 🕐 **10 Minutes**

Getting the right exercise prescription

Different people enjoy different types of activity. One person might love to take part in an organised team sport, whilst another may prefer non-competitive activities, such as hiking or canoeing. It's important to look for physical activities that you enjoy, as well as finding ways to bring more physical movement into your daily routine and reduce the amount of time spent staying still.

What is moderate to vigorous aerobic activity?

If you are doing moderate exercise, you will notice that your heart rate starts to increase and you are breathing faster and feeling warmer! Doing these activities can help to balance strong emotions, create feelings of happiness and wellbeing and boost your energy levels. Examples include:

→ brisk walking or hiking

→ cycling

→ bouncing on a trampoline

→ skateboarding or rollerblading

→ circuit training or high-intensity interval workouts

→ mowing the lawn

→ swimming

→ ball sports, like football, rugby, netball and hockey.

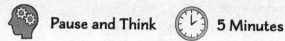

Pause and Think   **5 Minutes**

What examples of moderate or vigorous activity can you think of? What would you like to try if you had more time? Could you fit in a shorter activity to break up your busy day?

Activities that strengthen muscles and bones

Activities to improve muscle or bone strength, balance and flexibility often provide a great opportunity to connect socially and build friendships. They may also help with your concentration, focus and settling your busy mind, as well as building self-esteem as you see yourself achieving and developing new skills. Examples include:

→ gymnastics

→ martial arts

→ dance

→ rock climbing

→ yoga.

Pause and Think   **5 Minutes**

What examples of activities to strengthen your muscles and bones can you think of? What would you try if you had more time? Could you fit in a shorter activity to break up your busy day?

 **Read This** 🕐 **5 Minutes**

Reduce time spent sitting or lying down

It's important to spread activity through the day and cut down the length of time you spend sitting or lying down. There are many ways to do this, such as:

→ setting an alarm to remind you to get up and stretch your legs when studying

→ setting a goal for a daily number of steps using a pedometer

→ walking or cycling rather than taking a bus or car

→ getting off the bus a stop early to walk for a few minutes

→ keeping moving while you do your usual activities: going for a walk while talking on the phone, reading an article when standing up or listening to a podcast as you tidy your room.

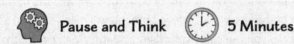 **Pause and Think** 🕐 **5 Minutes**

What can you try that might help you cut down the amount of time you spend sitting or lying down?

 **Try This** 🕐 **10 Minutes**

Tips to get moving

Here are some of our tips for getting moving and increasing your physical activity. Take a look at the chart below and make a note of what's most important to you and what you plan to try doing to improve your Healthy Activity Habits!

Tip for Healthy Activity Habits	What I will try
Start low and build up slowly: A brisk 10- or 15-minute walk can lead to a jog. Then gradually increase the speed and the distance.	
Make it social: Exercise with friends helps with motivation and enjoyment. Who can you enlist to join you at the gym or in a dance class?	

cont.

Tip for Healthy Activity Habits	What I will try
Remind yourself of the benefits: Picture yourself looking fitter and healthier, having more energy and focus. Accept compliments from others and give yourself some encouraging words to keep going.	
Take small steps to get prepared: Start by doing some research and finding out about local classes... getting the kit... making sure you can get a lift to the club... these are all small steps in the right direction.	

 Read This  10 Minutes

Healthy eating habits

Healthy eating is important for taking care of both the body and the mind. A healthy diet is essential for your body's growth and development, will help you keep a healthy weight and provides energy so you can enjoy your daily activities. Making healthy eating choices can boost your self-esteem, as you feel a sense of pride from knowing you are making active choices to take care of yourself. In the long-term, healthy eating habits can reduce your future risks of health conditions such as diabetes and heart disease.

What is healthy eating?

A healthy, balanced diet contains a range of foods from each of the different food groups. You don't need to achieve this with every meal, but it's helpful to try to find a balance over a day or even a week.

→ **Fruit and vegetables**: Aim for at least five portions of fruit and vegetables per day. These are a good source of vitamins, minerals and fibre and should make up around one third of your total food intake.

→ **Carbohydrates**: Starchy carbohydrates such as potatoes, bread, rice and pasta should also make up around one third of your intake and are a good source of energy. Try to include higher fibre varieties, such as wholewheat pasta, brown rice and wholemeal bread.

→ **Protein**: Foods high in protein include beans, pulses, fish, eggs and meat. Where possible, choose lean cuts of meat and reduce processed meats such as bacon, ham and sausages. Pulses, such as beans, peas and lentils, are great alternatives to meat and are low in fat and high in fibre and protein.

→ **Dairy foods,** such as milk, cheese and yoghurt, are good sources of protein and calcium. Aim for lower fat and lower sugar choices, or consider dairy alternatives, such as soya, especially when they are fortified with extra calcium.

→ **Fats and sugars**: Eating healthily involves cutting down on food and drinks high in fat, sugar and salt, such as fizzy drinks, crisps, cakes, biscuits and chocolate. This doesn't mean you have to give up all your favourite foods completely! But these foods should be eaten less often and in smaller amounts.

Unsaturated fats are healthier and include vegetable, olive and sunflower oils, although all types of fat are high in energy and should be eaten sparingly.

Balancing the different food groups

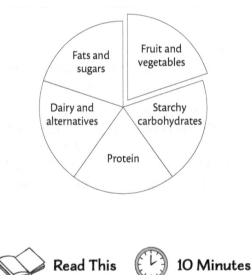

Read This **10 Minutes**

Getting the balance right – nutrients and minerals
Eating a varied and balanced diet should enable you to get all the energy and nutrients you need from the food and drink you consume. However, there are some important nutrients that will help you remain feeling healthy and full of energy.

If you feel run down or tired, you may be low on iron. Females are especially at risk because they lose iron during their period. You can get iron from foods such as red meat, breakfast cereals and bread.

Calcium and vitamin D keep bones and teeth healthy. We get most of our vitamin D from the sun, but it's also in some foods. Sources of calcium include milk, other dairy products and leafy green vegetables.

Stay hydrated

Aim to drink six to eight glasses of fluids a day – water and low-fat milk are both healthy choices. Try to cut down any sugary or caffeinated drinks, and don't drink more than 150ml (a small glass) per day of fruit juices or smoothies.

Create a healthy eating routine

It's helpful to eat regularly and to include a range of foods that provide a steady release of energy into the body and avoiding 'sugar spikes', which can affect your energy, mood, concentration and ability to learn. Try not to skip meals, especially breakfast, which helps set you up for the day ahead. Skipping meals won't help you lose weight and you may miss out on important nutrients.

Eating for happiness

Preparing food and eating together can be a way to connect with friends and family, which can make eating food a pleasure and an opportunity to appreciate and enjoy the moment. Try to continue making healthy eating choices, and seek out people who will support you in your healthy eating goals.

If you are feeling low or anxious, you may notice changes in your appetite or enjoyment of food. Some people turn to food as a comfort for emotional distress or as an energy boost, which can lead to cravings for sugary junk foods. These may be enjoyable in the short term but have unhealthy consequences if they become a repeated or frequent habit.

Eating disorders

Eating disorders are serious and increasingly common amongst young people, and they can affect your physical health, emotional wellbeing and how you live your life. Common eating disorders include anorexia nervosa, bulimia nervosa and binge eating.

If eating makes you feel anxious, guilty or upset, or you are restricting your food intake or changing your eating patterns because of emotional distress, it is important to talk about this with someone that you trust, as there are effective treatments available.

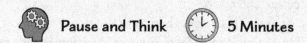

Pause and Think   **5 Minutes**

What are your current helpful and unhelpful eating habits?

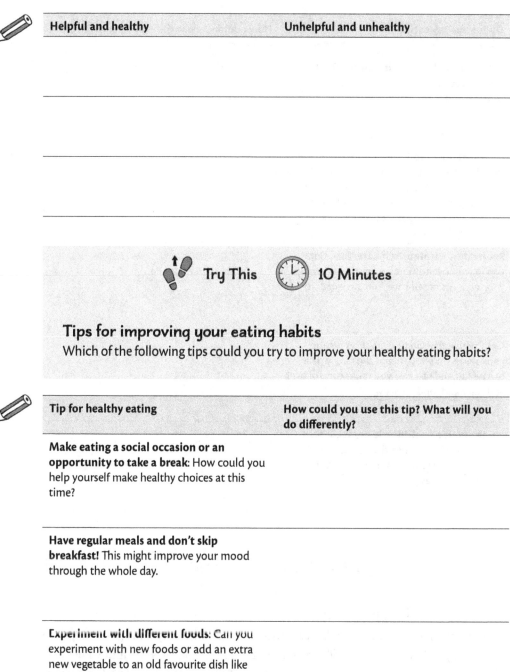

Helpful and healthy	Unhelpful and unhealthy

⒴ Try This   🕐 10 Minutes

Tips for improving your eating habits
Which of the following tips could you try to improve your healthy eating habits?

Tip for healthy eating	How could you use this tip? What will you do differently?
Make eating a social occasion or an opportunity to take a break: How could you help yourself make healthy choices at this time?	
Have regular meals and don't skip breakfast! This might improve your mood through the whole day.	
Experiment with different foods: Can you experiment with new foods or add an extra new vegetable to an old favourite dish like spaghetti bolognaise or curry? Be patient and don't give up! It can take a few attempts before you start to enjoy new flavours.	

cont.

Tip for healthy eating	How could you use this tip? What will you do differently?
Have a glass of water with meals: This helps hydrate you and may help to balance your appetite and food intake.	
Get rid of junk food: This will make it easier to resist when you are tired or hungry. Fill your cupboards with healthy snacks such as fruit, nuts, yoghurt and wholemeal bread. Keep biscuits and cakes as an occasional treat rather than a regular habit.	
See healthy eating as self-care: Each time you make a healthy choice, see this as giving yourself a gift of self-care. You are worth it!	
Get involved: Begin to plan, shop for and cook meals for yourself and the family. This can be fun and will give you more control over your diet and food choices.	
Think about a healthy role model: Who do you admire that has healthy eating habits? What can you learn from them? Can you use any of these ideas yourself?	

 Read This 10 Minutes

Other Unhealthy Life Habits

Many other aspects of everyday life can also become unhealthy and have a negative impact on your life and your wellbeing if they get out of balance with your values and other priorities. Substance and alcohol misuse can both cause physical and emotional damage. We will not go into detail here, but if you are affected, it's important to recognise the problem and seek help.

How we use technology

Our use of technology has changed hugely in recent years. We spend far more time online – working, studying, shopping, playing games, connecting with other people and even exercising in a virtual environment.

Living in this digital age brings many benefits, but spending too much time online, playing computer games or using social media can be very addictive. It can be hard to keep track or control how much time you are spending online, and it can be difficult to stop once you get started.

Technology use can start to become a problem if it's getting in the way of other important life activities. Much smartphone use involves frequent checking and short bursts of activity (Oulasvirta, Rattenbury and Raita 2012), so using phones can become a frequent habit that interferes with your concentration on other tasks.

We also know that overuse of technology can affect your productivity and memory, dampen creative thinking, increase stress and reduce your sleep quality. And it keeps you indoors – not moving and not gaining the benefits of regular physical movement.

So, the aim is to find a balance between use of technology and other important parts of your life by Following your Guide and keeping important priorities in mind as you make Wise choices about how to use your time.

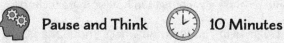 **Pause and Think** **10 Minutes**

How much time do you spend using technology or online?
Use the chart to calculate how much time you spend using technology during weekdays and at weekends.

How you interact	How much time each day (weekdays)?	How much time each day (weekends)?
Interacting online with people where you can see their face (e.g. FaceTime or video calls).		
Communicating via text messages or email.		
Social media or other group interactions online.		

cont.

How you interact	How much time each day (weekdays)?	How much time each day (weekends)?
Playing online games with other people.		
Spending time without interacting with others (e.g. playing computer games by yourself).		

Pause and Think ⏱ 5 Minutes

→ What do you notice? Do you think you have the balance about right?

→ Can you find ways to keep moving and avoid spending too long sitting or lying?

→ Are your technology habits getting in the way of other life priorities, or are you using it as a way of avoiding difficult feelings?

→ Do you need to make any changes in how you use technology?

→ Can your Guide help you focus on what's important to you and look for ways to find a balance of activities in all the areas of life that you care about?

....

....

....

Read This ⏱ 5 Minutes

Identifying unhelpful patterns

Maybe you have reached this section and are thinking: 'Actually, I think I'm OK. I have a healthy lifestyle, and this has made me realise I am doing fine!'

Or maybe you are caught up in a bit of a vicious cycle. If this is the case, you might find it helpful to step back and take a look at what's getting in the way of creating Healthy Life Habits.

Pause and Think 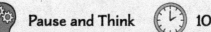 **10 Minutes**

Unhelpful thoughts and behaviour patterns

→ How do you feel when you are struggling with Unhealthy Life Habits?

→ What negative or unhelpful thoughts create an obstacle to forming Healthy Life Habits?

→ What patterns of behaviour do these unhelpful thoughts and feelings lead to?

→ What people or places help encourage you to change? Who and what stops you making progress?

→ How can this help you create more healthy patterns?

....

....

....

 Pause and Think  **10 Minutes**

Overcoming obstacles to Healthy Life Habits

In this final section, we will use your GROW skills to help you overcome any obstacles that might be getting in the way of creating Healthy Life Habits.

If you feel, think or do this...	Consider this...	What's important to you? How can you use this?
I can't get going with regular exercise – I just keep putting it off. That cake is too hard to resist. I'll start my healthy eating plan tomorrow.	**Use your Guide** and remind yourself why this is important. Think about overcoming procrastination: What would make it easier to start? For example, doing a class with a friend or picturing yourself in your new outfit.	

cont.

If you feel, think or do this...	Consider this...	What's important to you? How can you use this?
I can't be bothered. I feel too tired. I hate exercise – I'd rather read a book.	We sometimes don't feel like doing things but feel great afterwards. Try getting **Ready for Action**, take one small step and wait for the good feelings to catch up! Get prepared by putting your kit by the door. Can you alter your sleep patterns to feel more energised?	
I'm so unfit, I'll look ridiculous. I haven't played sport for ages – I'm useless at it.	Use **Open and Observing** skills to notice your inner critic stepping in. Be kind to yourself, and turn to your inner coach, using **Wise Mind** to help you plan helpful choices, actions and long-term gains. Maybe you focus first on healthy eating or reduce the time you are sitting still by taking a walk in nature or dancing to your favourite music while tidying your room.	
I've got too much else to do – I don't have time! I'm in the middle of this game – I can't go to sleep now!	Again, turn to your **Wise Mind**. Planning your time and creating a structure can help fit things in and reduce stress. Balance is important: work, rest and play. A 5- or 10-minute burst of activity can improve your focus and attention and help get more done. Be realistic about timings, allowing some breathing space and time for unexpected events.	

Planning your time using Wise Mind

Thinking that you don't have enough time is one of the commonest blocks to creating Healthy Life Habits. This can lead to stress and a feeling of overwhelm or make you feel despondent and give up trying.

Structuring your time wisely helps to get things done and can reduce stress and save time in the long run. Having a routine for some things and being flexible with others is also helpful in ensuring you use time effectively.

You may be the kind of person that creates a revision timetable and sticks to it, or you may create an elaborate plan and then do everything else that needs doing rather than the revision you planned. Or you may create a plan that is so demanding that healthy eating, sleeping, exercise and relaxation all go completely out of the window and your health suffers.

Planning your time is a key life skill. Using Wise Mind to **prioritise** is an important first step. That includes putting yourself and your health at the top of the list by doing things you know work for you and keep you well.

PRIORITISING AND USING A TO-DO LIST

Non-negotiables are activities or choices that go into your week whatever else is happening. You make the time and do them regularly, which turns them into a habit. This might include things like going to school or work, eating and sleeping. Parents or people around you may impose other things like household chores or homework.

There are other things that you have more choice over, but you can **choose** to turn other activities into your personal non-negotiables. This might include ways of looking after your health and wellbeing. You can decide to reduce or increase the time spent on them or how often you do them, but they are still part of your regular routine.

After planning your non-negotiables, you can make a to-do list and decide what else you want to achieve each day. Think about how **important** it is and whether it is **urgent**. Does it have to be done today and right now? Try to include no more than three priority items that are urgent for each day, after your non-negotiables. This ensures that you are more likely to achieve them and feel good about it rather than feeling disappointed or under pressure. Celebrate if you get the three things completed and have time to do something else that is less important!

REALISTIC SCHEDULING

It is also important to be realistic about how long things take and allow for events or opportunities that appear unexpectedly and take priority over what you planned to do. Life is never totally predictable! So, it helps not to cram too much into your to-do list and to leave gaps. Most of us are overambitious with time – we think we can do more than is possible in the time available and underestimate how long things actually take.

It also may help to remember that the average human can only concentrate for a maximum of 20 minutes at a time. If you lack sleep, are hungry, are stressed or emotional or have an attention problem, this is considerably reduced, so scheduling brief breaks and being realistic is important.

The way we move from having to consciously plan things to creating a Healthy Life Habit is simple: **repeat** + **repeat** + **repeat**! Make it a non-negotiable part of your routine.

Try This   **10 Minutes**

Time test experiment

Pick an activity that you really enjoy. Maybe going on social media or playing a video game. Set an alarm to go off after **5 minutes** and **stop** when the alarm goes off.

Review what happened and note it down. Were you surprised when the alarm went off? Did you manage to stop? How hard was it to resist the urge to continue? Did you manage to stop and if not, how much longer did you spend?

Pick a task that is important but that you perhaps don't enjoy. Maybe reading a chapter of a textbook in a subject you dislike. Plan in your head that you are going to do this for **5 minutes.** Start a stopwatch and then only look at it after you think 5 minutes has passed.

Review what happened and note it down. How long did you actually spend before you looked at your watch?

Pick a necessary everyday task, such as taking a shower and putting on your clothes, and estimate how long you think you will spend doing this. Start a stopwatch when you start the task and stop the stopwatch when you finish.

Your estimate:

Actual time the task took:

What did you discover from this time test experiment? How could you use this to bring healthy habits into your daily routine?

Jay was getting more and more upset and angry, and the rows with his parents had increased. His grades were sliding, and he was worried he might not get to college as he hoped if he didn't do better. He was tired and really fed up.

Jay took a few minutes to look back at some old photos in his phone – times when he had felt better and more himself. He saw himself smiling, looking fit and active, exercising with friends and doing well at school. He realised that his mood and confidence had been far higher when he was playing hockey, eating regular meals at home and sleeping well.

Jay was about to make some Wise choices and put some non-negotiables into his week. He decided to stop wasting hours on social media and gaming. Instead, he was going to get fitter, eat healthier and get his life back on track. He started by using a planner on his phone, setting some small exercise goals and planning them into his week. To get himself going on 'Project Jay', he started eating a healthy breakfast and walking to school at a brisk pace every morning to improve his focus and kickstart his day.

Try This   **10 Minutes**

Create a Healthy Life Habit

Follow these GROW steps to create your own Healthy Life Habit.

Use your Guide to motivate you and decide what's important. Which Healthy Life Habit will you plan to create? Think about how you would like to see yourself – now and in the future. Example: 'I picture myself healthy and fit with a career when I am 30. I love nature and animals, particularly my dog.'

Get Ready for Action: Set a realistic goal and some small steps towards it by planning your time in a way that keeps you feeling well and happy. Use your phone or a diary to plan your non-negotiables into your schedule for the week. Example: 'I am starting with a regular exercise plan and eating regularly. Week 1 I will walk/run for 20 minutes with the dog in the park three times per week in the mornings.'

Be Open and Observe any unhelpful patterns and acknowledge any difficult feelings. You can learn to surf the urge to give in to Unhealthy Life Habits and step back from thoughts that create obstacles to you moving towards your healthy life plan. Be flexible and adapt where you can or problem-solve any difficulties. Example: 'I will put my alarm on the other side of the room and leave my kit ready to make it more likely that I will do this. I will stroke the dog and be in the moment, appreciating nature when in the park.'

Make Wise choices about how to spend your time. How can you resist the urge to give in to unhealthy patterns? Listen to your inner coach, making Wise choices when planning your time and continuing Wise actions regularly until they form a pattern in your life. Make an 'If… Then Plan' to overcome challenges or create a Healthy Rule. Example: 'If it is raining… then I will do a class instead of a run; If my friends are eating junk food… then I will choose the healthier option.' Review your plans and adjust if necessary.

Time it... Schedule it... Do it... Repeat it to create a Healthy Life Habit!

What we have covered in Chapter 10: Healthy Life Habits

→ We looked at some facts and information about sleep, physical activity and healthy eating.

→ We looked at some of the unhelpful thoughts, feelings and behaviours that create Unhealthy and Healthy Life Habits.

→ We explored some other unhelpful habits, including overuse of technology, and some tips for overcoming problems and challenges.

→ We identified which GROW skills you can use to create your own personal healthy life plan.

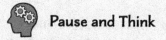 **Pause and Think** **5 Minutes**

→ What are the most important messages for you from this chapter?

→ What have you learned or understood after reading it and trying the exercises?

....

....

....

 ## Taking action

→ What are you going to do differently now?

→ What are your next steps?

→ What will you practise on a regular basis in order to build on what you have learned?

....

....

....

Chapter 11

SURVIVING SETBACKS

→ Do you have trouble bouncing back after some of the ups and downs of daily life?

→ Has a difficult life event knocked your confidence, making it harder to keep going?

→ Are you worried you might forget what you've learned and slip back to square one?

→ Learn to create your own personal Setback Survival Plan! Read on…

 **Read This**   **10 Minutes**

Using your skills and Surviving Setbacks

It feels great when things are working out and everything seems to be going your way. But life rarely stays straightforward and problem-free for long! For most of us, sooner or later some kind of problem or difficulty will come along – and you will have to choose whether to ride over the bump, find a way around it or allow it to stop you in your tracks.

Life is full of uncertainty, and it's just not possible to predict or plan for every possible problem or setback that we might be faced with. But over time, we can learn to accept this and to develop flexibility as we adjust to changing circumstances.

Developing resilience involves finding ways to adapt and bounce back in the face of adversity and challenges and problems, whilst remaining true to the person that you really want to be.

Being more resilient does not automatically mean feeling more happy or relaxed. It may involve coping or getting through a challenging or stressful situation and still standing at the end of the day. And over time, you might start to develop a sense of pride in your ability to cope with challenges, starting to see it as a sign of inner strength, independence and determination. This doesn't mean that you won't feel frustrated or discouraged at times but that you don't allow these distressing thoughts and feelings to prevent you from looking for ways to work through and move on from the problem.

What is a setback?

A setback is anything that gets in the way of your plans, your wellbeing or your happiness, such as:

→ a period of illness or injury – emotional or physical

→ a disappointing event, such as not achieving the grades you were expecting or not being offered the job you were really hoping for

→ coping with changing circumstances, such as moving home or school

→ problems in the wider world that we have no control over, such as the pandemic and changes with the exam system.

How we cope with these different types of setbacks will depend on how much control we have over the problem. We'll think more about this as the chapter progresses.

Skills for Surviving Setbacks

As with all things, Surviving Setbacks takes time and practice. Some of the key skills that will build resilience and enable you to bounce back from setbacks include: seeking help when you need it, finding ways to solve problems, being able to notice and learn from mistakes, being kind to yourself when you are facing disappointment or loss and accepting that there are some things in life that nobody is able to control.

We are hoping that by now you are starting to use some of the skills you have learned in this book so far, and you might already have some ideas about how to survive, and even thrive, in the face of a setback. In the rest of the chapter, we will look at ways to use your GROW skills to overcome setbacks, including how to:

→ Follow your Guide by reminding you of your personal values, skills and strengths, and what is important to you

→ be Ready for Action – this includes making plans to cope, solve or overcome problems, and taking actions that increase your competence and confidence or provide you with structure and security

→ be Open and Observe your emotions and needs in challenging times, showing self-care and making use of support. Use noticing skills and awareness to ride the waves of distress without feeling overwhelmed by your emotions

→ use your Wise Mind to help you adopt a GROWth Mindset and choose coping strategies that are likely to help you overcome any setbacks. This includes learning from mistakes, getting support from people that you trust and listening to your inner coach.

We will use this to help you choose what works for you, build on your past successes and create your own personal **Setback Survival Plan**.

Pause and Think **5 Minutes**

→ What challenges, problems or setbacks are you facing at the moment?

....

....

....

Read This **5 Minutes**

Ask your Guide for directions!
When facing setbacks and difficulties, you can turn to your Guide to remind yourself what you care about most and what values might be important to focus on. This helps give life a sense of purpose, meaning and perspective, and reminds you how you want to live as a person, no matter what life throws at you.

Ready for Action!
A simple step when facing any kind of problem or difficulty is to plan a micro-action that moves you in the direction of one of your key values.

This action might help you to solve one or more of the problems you are facing.

And even if it doesn't, taking any kind of active step that's linked to one of your important values is likely to help lift your mood and remind you that you still have choices, even when facing major difficulties.

And as a kind of domino effect, this micro-action could trigger all kinds of other possibilities and changes that **are** related to the problem in your life.

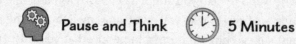 **Pause and Think** **5 Minutes**

Read through the chart below and add some of your own examples.

Value	Micro-action	Can I link this action to my problem?
Creativity	I will spend 5 minutes doing some mindful colouring today.	I felt calmer and more able to think clearly afterwards, which helped me come up with some new ideas.
Friendship	I will go for a walk with my friend.	I was able to tell my friend what's been happening, and I felt very relieved to have someone to talk to.

 **Read This** **5 Minutes**

The importance of choice

No matter how difficult the problem or situation that you are facing is, remember that you always have a choice about which action to take next. You may not be able to solve the problem directly, but you **do** have choices about how to respond to it. This is true no matter what circumstances you are coping with.

You might use your Wise Mind to help you choose what's most likely to be helpful. We talk more about this later in the chapter, but for now...

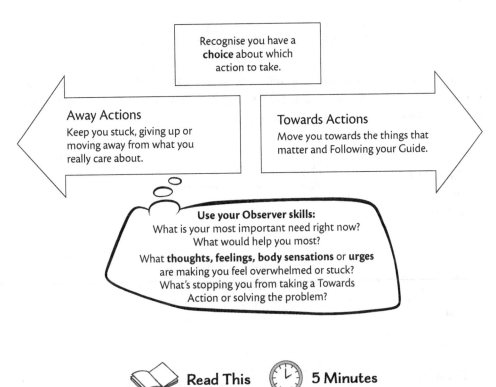

Recognise you have a **choice** about which action to take.

Away Actions
Keep you stuck, giving up or moving away from what you really care about.

Towards Actions
Move you towards the things that matter and Following your Guide.

Use your Observer skills:
What is your most important need right now?
What would help you most?
What **thoughts, feelings, body sensations** or **urges** are making you feel overwhelmed or stuck?
What's stopping you from taking a Towards Action or solving the problem?

Read This   **5 Minutes**

Finding your choices

Here are some of the many different types of activity that you might try in different situations:

Calm and soothing actions	• Give a sense of calm or enjoyment. • Reduce stress. • Connect with your five senses. • Sleep, food, rest, exercise.
Connecting and grounding actions	• Remind you of who and what are most important. • Connect you with people that you trust. • Connect you with your values. • Provide a sense of safety and security.
Boosting or releasing actions	• Sharing thoughts and feelings. • Releasing tension and frustration. • Clarifying the problem. • Allowing others to take care of you.

Pause and Think  **5 Minutes**

Which activities are most useful in different circumstances? Which are most in line with your values? What can you **choose** to do next time you are facing a setback or problem? Complete the chart with some of your own ideas.

Calm and soothing actions	• *Example: Take a relaxing shower.* • What are your ideas? When could you use these? • •
Connecting and grounding actions	• *Example: Talk to someone you trust.* • What are your ideas? When could you use these? • •
Boosting or releasing actions	• *Example: Going for a brisk 5-minute walk.* • What are your ideas? When could you use these? • •

 **Read This** **3 Minutes**

Be Open and Observe how you are feeling
Soothing distress

When your mind is churning over all sorts of unhelpful and distressing thoughts about the problems you are facing, making you feel stressed, anxious and upset, you are likely to find it much harder to see the bigger picture or to solve problems. As we discovered in Chapter 5, when your emotions are high, and your threat and alarm systems are overactive, your higher brain does not work as efficiently, so it's harder to think clearly and reason through complex situations.

 **Try This** **10 Minutes**

Shift into your physical body

If you are overwhelmed by distress from a painful life experience, try shifting out of your mind and emotions and into your physical body, which can help calm your mind and shift your stress response down a gear, helping you to feel calmer and more grounded.

Try it out! Take a shower, go for a walk or a run, dance, bounce on a trampoline, do some yoga or practise your ball skills. Notice what happens to your body and mind.

Just 5–10 minutes of focusing on the physical sensations of movement can help reduce your inner sense of pressure and release some of the emotional tension.

Afterwards, choose what would be the most helpful thing to do next… and move on to doing this with as much attention as you can.

 **Read This** **5 Minutes**

Notice and name what's happening

Even small setbacks can sometimes trigger strong feelings, such as frustration, disappointment, hurt or loss. This is completely normal and it's important to acknowledge that your feelings are real and completely valid. When you are facing a problem or setback, it's often not necessary to rush into problem-solving, and it may be more helpful to take some time to notice what's going on inside you.

The first step is to recognise what's happening, using Open and Observe skills to notice and name the thoughts and feelings that have popped up. It can also be helpful to shift your attention out of the worry thoughts in your mind, focusing your attention on your body or your five senses to create some space that allows you to make Wise decisions about how to tackle the situation. You can turn back to Chapter 3 for a reminder of how to do this.

You could also share how you are feeling with a trusted supporter or friend or write it down in a journal. This process of recognising and naming what's happening inside helps create some perspective on problems and may help you to gradually work through difficult emotions so that they have less impact on your subsequent thoughts and actions.

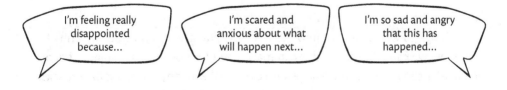

I'm feeling really disappointed because…

I'm scared and anxious about what will happen next…

I'm so sad and angry that this has happened…

 **Try This** 1 Minute

Quick five senses for overwhelm

If you are feeling overwhelmed by strong thoughts and feelings, take one minute to connect with two or three of your senses for 20–30 seconds each. Choose from these options.

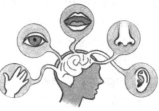

→ **Sight**: Look around and notice one colour that's around you. Name two or three things you can see with this colour. Repeat with another colour.

→ **Sound**: Pause and notice the loudest background sound and the quietest. Can you hear yourself breathing?

→ **Taste**: If you are eating or drinking, pause and pay attention to the taste, temperature and texture of what you are consuming.

→ **Smell**: Are there any smells around you, even very faint ones?

→ **Touch**: Wriggle your toes on the ground, feel your seat on the chair, rub your hands together or stretch your arms wide, just noticing the physical sensations of being alive.

→ **Finish by asking yourself**: What feelings or emotions can I notice? What thoughts are going through my mind? What's the most helpful next thing that I can do?

 **Read This** 5 Minutes

Take care of yourself and your needs

Using your Observe skills might also involve noticing that you need to take care of some basic health needs for sleep, nutritious food and general self-care before you can focus on other things. You can look at Chapter 10 for some tips on how to do this.

Stay connected to the people that matter

When things go wrong, it's common to react by hiding away and disconnecting from the people we care about. But this can make you more isolated, meaning it becomes even harder to find the emotional resources to deal with any problems or setbacks.

An important skill for coping with setbacks is to find ways to stay connected with the people you care about. Knowing that you are not alone may provide the strength you need to cope with your problems.

This might involve giving others the chance to support you, perhaps by opening up and asking someone you trust for help. Or it might simply involve deepening your friendship with another person and allowing this to act as a source of strength that you can draw on as you go through the process of coping with life's difficulties.

 **Pause and Think** 🕐 **5 Minutes**

When you are faced by problems or difficulties, do you tend to pull away or turn towards people? Who might you turn to? Can you think of any way(s) to strengthen your connections with people you care about when facing a difficult situation?

 **Read This** 🕐 **5 Minutes**

Being a friend to yourself

When things go wrong, many people react with self-criticism and can start to think negatively and blame themselves for the problem. You might start calling yourself names, saying things like: 'You idiot! Why did you let this happen?'. But this negative self-talk makes matters worse, as it leads to low mood, dents your self-esteem and undermines your attempts to solve the problem.

We talk about self-criticism in more detail in Chapter 6 on low mood, so if this is something that you recognise, you could look here for ideas of how to change this thinking habit.

Instead, can you become a friend, coach or supporter to yourself? Try out one of the short practices that can help develop your own sense of self-care and self-compassion.

 **Pause and Think** 🕐 **5 Minutes**

You are not alone

If you are facing a setback or problem, take a moment to think about all the people across the country, and even across the world, who might be coping with a similar difficulty. If you are feeling lonely after a break-up or a relationship or frustrated by problems that feel out of your control, feeling embarrassed after making a mistake or whatever the problem that you are facing is, try to remember that there are many other people who are likely to be feeling the same way.

Can you send out a sense of well-wishing and kindness to everyone who is struggling with this? Can you find a sense of compassion and care and imagine sharing this feeling with everyone who needs it? Can you offer support and understanding, without slipping into any kind of judgement or blame?

And can you include yourself in this group, as one person amongst many others who are struggling for similar reasons? Can you offer yourself the same care and support that you can offer to others?

Seek comfort from your surroundings

Seek out a place that feels calming or comforting to you and spend a few minutes here.

It might be walking or sitting in the garden, snuggling in bed in your most comfortable pyjamas or curled up on the sofa, listening to your favourite music. You might choose to cuddle up with a pet, a soft toy or a squashy pillow for warmth and comfort and allow the closeness and physical touch to gradually soothe and comfort you in these difficult times.

Wish yourself well

Sit quietly and place one hand on your heart or put a hand on each shoulder and give yourself a gentle hug. Allow feelings of warmth and care for yourself to surround and fill your body.

Try telling yourself: 'This is a tough moment. This is really hard and maybe it's not very fair. I can wish myself well and be kind to myself because I really need someone on my side right now.'

What other friendly or encouraging words can you say? Try to choose one or two phrases that have meaning for you. For example: 'I care for you [say your own name]. I wish the best for you.'

Wise Mind

In this next section, we will look at what attitudes, beliefs and mindsets might help when you are dealing with problems and difficulties.

 **Read This** **5 Minutes**

Do you have a Fixed or a GROWth Mindset?

Your mindset can have a big influence on how you react when things go wrong. There are two types of mindset: a Fixed Mindset and a GROWth Mindset.

People with a Fixed Mindset take the view that you cannot change your intelligence or your ability to achieve – it's just something that you are born with... or not! So, if you make a mistake or find something difficult, this means that you are just not up to the task and should probably give up. Having a Fixed Mindset often leads to people becoming afraid of failure and doing everything they can to avoid it, either by not trying or by not taking on challenging tasks.

People with a GROWth Mindset see things very differently. They recognise that our brains can grow stronger with time and effort. This means that with practice and effort, you can learn to do almost anything! Because of this understanding, people with a GROWth Mindset are excited by challenge. They are also usually less concerned about failure, as they see it as just a temporary setback and the starting point for developing new abilities and skills. Even when they are disappointed, people with a GROWth Mindset are likely to remain optimistic and find it easier to bounce back from difficulties, believing they are capable of success if they keep working at it.

 **Pause and Think** **5 Minutes**

Comparing Fixed and GROWth Mindsets

Take a look at the following chart... do you tend towards a Fixed or a GROWth Mindset?

Fixed Mindset	GROWth Mindset
I find it hard to keep focused on long or complicated projects.	I try hard to finish most tasks and don't give up, even if it's difficult.
This isn't going well... I give up!	I'll try a different strategy... or ask for help.
I only like doing things that I'm already good at!	I love a difficult challenge!
I can't do this easily... I'll never be able to do it!	This might take some time! Can I find someone to help me learn...?
Mistakes are embarrassing! It's best to pretend I haven't made one.	I don't mind making mistakes... they help me learn!
I tried really hard and it still didn't work out! It must be my fault.	This might take time and effort but every step in the right direction is important.
It wasn't exactly right... I hate getting it wrong!	I'm aiming for progress, not perfection!

cont.

Fixed Mindset	GROWth Mindset
If someone is clever then they don't need to try very hard.	You get good at things by working hard at them... and you can always improve!
Plan A didn't work.	There's always plan B (and plan C, D and E...!).

What did you notice? You might have a mixture of both mindsets or it may depend on your mood and the type of task or situation. Does it make a difference if you are facing an educational task, a practical task, a sport or physical challenge or a creative challenge? This is completely normal! Make a note of your thoughts here:

 Pause and Think 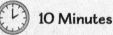 **10 Minutes**

GROW your GROWth Mindset

Even if you don't naturally have a GROWth Mindset, there are many ways to develop one. Take a look at the following tips.

Tip for a GROWth Mindset	How can you use this tip? What will you do differently?
Your brain learns through practice Your brain is strong, smart and capable of amazing things, and it can keep on learning and developing new connections throughout your life. Every time you learn or practise something, you're taking your brain for a strengthening workout! So, the more you learn, and the trickier the challenges you face are, the stronger your brain will grow.	
Keep trying Working hard towards a goal and being persistent are the most important skills that will eventually lead to success. In a difficult task, try not to focus on the outcome but instead think about the next steps, and keep putting in effort, trying not to give up even if things seem very hard. You can get there if you keep trying!	

Change the meaning of success

With a GROWth Mindset, success is less about proving that you're smart or talented and is more about stretching yourself to learn something new. So, being willing to grow, facing a difficult situation, being brave enough to try for the things that you really care about... these are the greatest signs of success.

Learn from others

If you are feeling stuck, unsure about how to approach a tricky question or life situation, it can help to turn to someone supportive, who may have different experience or knowledge to you. You might watch what they do or ask for encouragement or help. You might need to be willing to change or experiment with what you are doing, based on their feedback and suggestions.

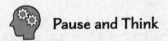 Pause and Think 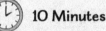 10 Minutes

I can't do it... YET

Sometimes, the way we think about our abilities can limit us or stop us from trying. But a GROWth Mindset can help you to realise that if you are willing to put in time and effort, you can learn to do just about anything! So, next time you think, 'I can't do it,' just add in one word: YET.

Saying, 'I can't do it YET,' will help you to see your challenge as a journey and encourage you to think about the steps you need to take to tackle it. For example:

> I can't draw people... YET = optimistic
> This answer isn't right... YET = encouraging
> I can't play the piano... YET = **GROWth Mindset**

In the following chart, list some of the things that you can't do... YET, and then try to think about what the first small step might be to help you change this.

What can't I do... YET?	What's the first small step to changing this?
Example: I can't swim 100 lengths of the swimming pool... YET!	I will start by trying to swim one length very slowly and rest at the end. I can build up gradually!

cont.

What can't I do... YET?	What's the first small step to changing this?

 **Read This** 🕐 **5 Minutes**

Seek your strengths!

Part of Surviving Setbacks involves recognising and building on your personal strengths and positive qualities, helping you to stay strong and determined in the face of life's obstacles.

We started thinking about your strengths and personal qualities in Chapter 8 on confidence. If you did the exercise on page 181, flip back now and review your answers, and see if you can add some new or different qualities to the list, focusing on strengths that might be extra helpful for coping with setbacks. Or this might be a great time to complete the activity if you haven't done it so far.

Now let's think about some of the skills and personal qualities that can help when coping with setbacks.

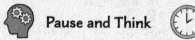 **Pause and Think** 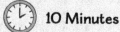 **10 Minutes**

Find your Surviving Setbacks skills

Can you identify an area in your life in which you have stuck with an activity for a while? Perhaps it's something you do regularly because you enjoy it or you are committed to doing it. It doesn't have to be anything complicated but ideally it's something that you have kept going for a while, such as a regular hobby, sport or activity, caring for a pet, a job, volunteering, education or learning.

In the next exercise, we will think about some of the skills in Surviving Setbacks that you already possess.

Activity	Example	What is your experience?
What activity have you kept up for a while?	I always manage to take my dog for a walk, even when I feel really fed up.	
What are some of the difficulties you run into in doing this activity? What gets in the way?	Sometimes it's raining, I'm running late or I'm just not in the mood.	
Which one of these is a common problem?	I'm often not in the mood to go, especially after a busy day.	
Can you think of any times in the past few weeks when that happened but you managed to do the activity anyway?	Yesterday morning, I was late getting up and it was quite dark outside. I really didn't want to go.	
On this occasion, what kept you going, despite the difficulty or obstacle?	The look on my dog's face. He was so excited to go and I couldn't let him down.	
Who or what else helps you to keep going with this despite some of the obstacles?	My sister sometimes comes with me and it's fun to chat while we walk.	
What are the benefits (to you and to others) of doing the activity?	My dog loves it and it keeps me fit. It helps me feel less stressed.	

Reflection

→ What can you learn from this?

→ What Surviving Setbacks skills have you found from your answers? What personal qualities have you discovered?

→ How could you use this to help you cope with any problems or setbacks that you are facing?

....

....

....

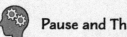 **Pause and Think**  **10 Minutes**

Create a Surviving Setbacks Superhero

Next, you will create your own avatar or superhero that represents how you would like to go about facing setbacks and difficulties.

Create your Surviving Setbacks Superhero	Examples	Your notes and ideas
Strengths Choose words from this list, or add your own, that highlight some important qualities you would like to remember when facing setbacks.	Flexible, courageous, persistent, encouraging, resourceful, caring, capable, positive, strong, adventurous, creative, unstoppable... Add your own ideas and words:	

People or characters that inspire you Can you think of a character or person (real or imagined) that captures these qualities? How do they cope with setbacks? What inspiring message or soundbite would they give?	A tennis player who showed huge determination and came back to win after being two sets down in the final. An inspiring hero or movie character who overcomes huge challenges. My friend who is in a wheelchair and plays basketball. Never give up or give in!
Places that inspire you Is there a place (real or imagined) that inspires these qualities in you?	Climbing up the sand dunes and looking out at the sea, feeling the fresh air. I feel I have achieved something and am rewarded by the great view.
Resilient actions What actions would your character encourage you to take? What would they do when faced by setbacks?	He would tell me to slow down, make a plan, get some help, keep trying and think carefully about what to try without panicking. He would want me to keep trying until I finish the task.
What does your Surviving Setbacks Superhero **look like?** Finish by creating a visual image for the character. What do they look like? What's their name? It might be the same name as the character who inspires you or something else.	I see my superhero as a powerful bird flying over the ocean, who never gives up until they reach their destination.

 **Read This**  **5 Minutes**

Survival Skills – Stay Standing in the face of problems

The next step is to follow your Surviving Setbacks Superhero's lead to help you 'Stay Standing' in the face of a setback. Your goal is to stay strong and keep going – this is even more important than having success in solving or overcoming problems.

You can even start to see negative life events and problems as opportunities to practise your Surviving Setbacks skills! This viewpoint turns life into a 'win-win' experience. If things go well, you win. If things do not go well, you have another chance to 'win' by being resilient. This can encourage you to embrace rather than avoid challenges and reduces your frustration when things are not going so well.

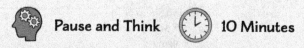 **Pause and Think** 🕐 **10 Minutes**

Testing your Surviving Setbacks Skills

Complete the chart below to plan how to Stay Standing when facing the next setback or challenge using your Surviving Setbacks Superhero.

Choose a situation
What situation will you choose to test out
your Surviving Setbacks skills?
Be specific: Who? Where? When?

**Ask your Surviving Setbacks Superhero
for advice**
What would be the wisest and most
sensible advice that they would give you?
What would be their attitude? What images
or ideas might help you to use these skills?

What actions can you take?
What choices do you have? What is most
likely to be helpful and move you towards
one (or more) of your important values?
What 'resilient actions' can you choose?

Prompts and reminders
How can you remember to follow your
Surviving Setbacks Superhero's advice?
What might help you to keep going in the
face of challenges or difficulties?

 **Read This**  **5 Minutes**

Practical problem-solving

It is helpful to break down and understand your reactions to setbacks and problems using a CBT framework, like we have in other chapters. We can also use the acronym **FACE** to think about some of the specific strategies that help us find courage and the ability to cope.

→ **F**ocus on things that you can control.

→ **A**cknowledge and allow feelings without being overwhelmed or stifled by them.

→ **C**onnect with your values, strengths and support, and the familiar, good things in your life.

→ **E**xpand your possibilities by looking to explore alternatives and use problem-solving.

Alice comes from a successful medical family. She holds strong values about achievement, as well as contribution and care for others. She is a hard-working student, who was hoping to go to university to study medicine. She enjoys keeping fit and being with friends, and she de-stresses by stroking and going on walks with her dog Benny and meeting and chatting with her friends Maria and Parvin.

Trigger event/setback: *Alice went to school to receive her exam results and was optimistic and excited. But when she looked at the results, she discovered that they did not meet the entry requirements to study medicine at the university of her choice.*

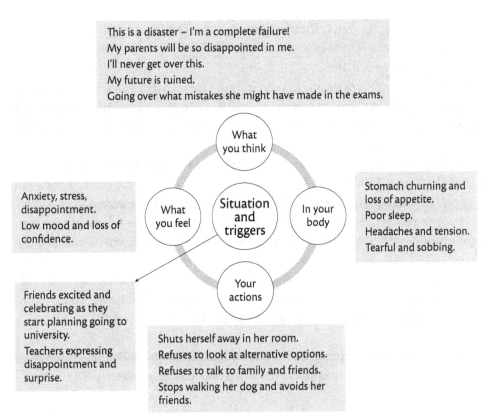

This is a disaster – I'm a complete failure!
My parents will be so disappointed in me.
I'll never get over this.
My future is ruined.
Going over what mistakes she might have made in the exams.

What you think

Situation and triggers

In your body

What you feel

Your actions

Anxiety, stress, disappointment.
Low mood and loss of confidence.

Stomach churning and loss of appetite.
Poor sleep.
Headaches and tension.
Tearful and sobbing.

Friends excited and celebrating as they start planning going to university.
Teachers expressing disappointment and surprise.

Shuts herself away in her room.
Refuses to look at alternative options.
Refuses to talk to family and friends.
Stops walking her dog and avoids her friends.

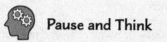 **Pause and Think**  **10 Minutes**

→ What can Alice **F**ocus on that is within her control?

→ What feelings can you identify with? What can she **A**cknowledge and what coping skills can she use to stop feeling overwhelmed and stifled?

→ Who could she **C**onnect with to get support and what could she connect with to ground herself?

→ How can she **E**xpand her possibilities and explore her options going forward?

. . . .

. . . .

. . . .

 **Read This** **10 Minutes**

Steps in problem-solving

Once you can think more clearly, you can start to focus on what you are able to change about a situation and use your problem-solving skills. You may also need to accept some things you cannot change, particularly past events or situations or other people's reactions or feelings.

If your mind is getting stuck on problems that don't have a solution, such as thinking endlessly about things that haven't happened yet, you can turn to Chapter 7 on anxiety for ideas of how to cope with mental preoccupation and worry.

For practical problems that do have possible solutions, there is a simple five-step problem-solving method. This can also help with decision-making and difficult choices.

STEP 1: NAME THE PROBLEM

What is the problem that you are facing? Try to be specific about what you are concerned about and decide if it is a problem you can solve or change.

Alice's example: *'I didn't get good enough grades for my university of choice to study the course that I wanted to do, so my application was rejected.'*

STEP 2: CREATE A BRAINSTORM – LIST IDEAS FOR SOLUTIONS

Next, list all the options or solutions that pop into your head. If you can, ask other people to help you think about as many possibilities as you can. Be as imaginative and creative as possible; don't worry about how unlikely the solutions might be at this stage, but keep in mind your Guide and your most important values.

Alice's possible solutions:

- *Take a year out, live on a kibbutz, resit in the autumn, redo the whole year.*

- *Change university, change course, change career choice, apply to a course in another country.*

- *Challenge the grades.*

STEP 3: LOOK AT THE PROS AND CONS

Next, choose the two or three options or solutions that most appeal and might have the best chance of success, and examine these further. Think of things for and against each option and what resources, further information or help you might need to choose the best option.

Possible solution	What's positive or helpful about this?	What might be the drawbacks or problems?	What extra help, information or resources do I need? What are the next steps?
Appeal my grades	I have done well through the year and in my mocks. Perhaps I could improve my grades this way.	The appeal may lose. Time is against me and they may not hold my place at uni.	I could ask the head of year at school for her opinion. Check whether uni will hold the place whilst I appeal. Speak to Dad to see if he can help me decide.
Take a year out	This would give me a chance to fulfil two of my important values: travel and nature. I could volunteer on a nature project and get some life experience, which might help my career later.	I have never been abroad alone and might feel homesick. This could be expensive.	Money – could I fundraise? It will take time to organise and arrange a trip. I need my parents' support and agreement.

cont.

Possible solution	What's positive or helpful about this?	What might be the drawbacks or problems?	What extra help, information or resources do I need? What are the next steps?
Other options...			

STEP 4: CHOOSE A SOLUTION

The next step is to choose your preferred option. You can then break down the solution you have chosen into small action steps and carry them out. It's also important to have a plan B (and maybe even a plan C, D and E!) as backups in case there are other obstacles to overcome.

Alice's example: Alice made an appointment to see her head of year, who was very supportive and realistic. She acknowledged how hardworking Alice was and helped her think about the pressure Alice sometimes placed on herself to achieve. What was the cost of that in terms of her enjoyment and quality of life? The teacher reminded Alice of all the other skills and qualities she had and the range of subjects she was good at. She advised her that the gap between the grades Alice received and those she needed was wide and it was unlikely that all three exams could be re-marked to get her the desired grades. She gave her the details of the careers advisor, who might be able to advise on other universities and options.

STEP 5: TRY YOUR SOLUTION AND NOTICE WHAT HAPPENS

The final step is to try out your preferred solution and notice what effect this has. Afterwards, you will need to think about any new obstacles or steps that you are aware of and think of ways to overcome these. If necessary, return to Step 1 and try a different solution.

In the next section, we have incorporated these problem-solving steps and some other skills into our complete Setback Survival Plan!

> **Alice reconnects**: After a difficult night with little sleep, no food and lots of tears, Alice finally allowed her sister Sarah and her mum into her room. Her mum made Alice's favourite drink and they talked about how Alice felt and her fears for the future. Sarah and her mum listened carefully, without judging, criticising or trying to problem-solve the situation too early.
>
> They reassured Alice that she was safe and loved and that they would support her in any way she chose. Her sister suggested they take the dog for a walk in the woods. Alice started to feel calmer. She was able to think more clearly and make sense of the situation. She reminded herself of her Guide and her values — to achieve, but more importantly, to care for others. She noticed how nature soothed her and how good this felt. She was ready to focus on what she could change about the situation and start to make plans.

Develop a Setback Survival Plan

Is there a problem or setback you have been grappling with or avoiding? How could you FACE the problem? Let's review the skills we have covered to overcome obstacles and Survive the Setback:

What is the situation, obstacle or setback? Briefly summarise what's happening and what's difficult about this situation.

Focus on your values and what you can control: What are your values and priorities in this situation? What direction is your Guide pointing? What are your personal skills, strengths and resources you can call upon? What are the parts of the situation that you can control?

Acknowledge what's happening: Be Open and Observe the thoughts, feelings, body sensations and urges to react that arise as you think about this situation. Use a CBT framework to help with this. Next, use your five senses or awareness of your body to soothe and calm strong feelings and reduce overwhelm. Be a kindly and supportive friend to yourself and offer yourself understanding and care rather than judgement or blame in the face of this difficult situation.

Choice and connection: As you prepare to take action, keep in mind that you can **choose** how to respond to challenges and setbacks. What might be a helpful small action that would be in line with your values? Can you seek support and connection rather than pulling away from people that you care about?

Expand your outlook: How could your Wise Mind help you face this situation? This could include:

→ tapping into your GROWth Mindset and actions: focusing on effort, persistence and making the next small step

→ remembering your surviving strengths and personal qualities by thinking about characters, places and people that inspire you – what would your Surviving Setbacks Superhero say? Can you connect with this image for support and encouragement?

→ finding ways to bring creativity and humour into how you approach this challenging situation.

Now, are you ready to move on to the problem-solving plan?

Step 1: Name the problem
What is the problem you are facing? Make sure you choose something that you can control or change.

....

....

....

Step 2: Brainstorm ideas for solutions

Make a list of as many ideas for solutions as possible. Be creative and think 'outside the box'.

....

....

....

Step 3: Look at the pros and cons

Choose three options and list the things **for** and **against** each option and your next steps.

....

....

....

Possible solution	What's positive or helpful about this?	What might be the drawbacks or problems?	What extra help, information or resources do you need? What are the next steps?

Step 4: Choose a solution and try it out

Pick your preferred option to try first and break this down into small steps or micro-actions. Be specific: What will you do? When? Where? Who could help?

....

....

....

Step 5: Notice what happens and keep going

What was the effect of your action? What can you learn from this? Are there any new obstacles? How could you overcome these? What will you try next? If needed, return to Step 1 and try a different solution.

What we have covered in Chapter 11: Surviving Setbacks

→ Setbacks are common and happen to everyone! Surviving Setbacks is about focusing on skills for Staying Standing and keeping going in the face of life's obstacles, challenges and difficulties.

→ Some of the most important skills for Surviving Setbacks include:

> making active choices about how to respond to setbacks that Follow your Guide and your important values

> taking a supportive, friendly and encouraging attitude towards yourself, without slipping into judgement or blame

> staying connected to the people that matter most to you

> recognising and building on your existing strengths and personal qualities

> asking your personal Surviving Setbacks Superhero for helpful advice

> bringing creativity and humour into how you approach the situation

> following the five steps of the problem-solving plan as you work through problems and seek solutions.

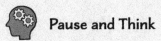 **Pause and Think**  **5 Minutes**

→ What are the most important messages for you from this chapter?

→ What have you learned or understood after reading it and trying the exercises?

....

....

....

Taking action

→ What are you going to do differently now?

→ What actions will you take as a result of reading this chapter?

→ Are there any regular actions or patterns of behaviour that you might try to practise or develop?

....

....

....

....

....

....

....

....

References and Resources

We would like to acknowledge the following books and articles, which have influenced the writing of this book.

Bennett, R. and Oliver, J. (2019) *Acceptance and Commitment Therapy: 100 Key Points and Techniques.* Routledge.

David, L. (2006) *Using CBT in General Practice: The 10 Minute Consultation.* Scion.

Davies, S. C. (2014) *Annual Report of the Chief Medical Officer 2013, Public Mental Health Priorities: Investing in the Evidence.* London: Department of Health.

Dweck, C. (2007) *Mindset: The New Psychology of Success.* Ballantine Books.

Evans-Lacko, S., Aguilar-Gaxiola, S., Al-Hamzawi, A., Alonso, J., *et al.* (2018). 'Socio-economic variations in the mental health treatment gap for people with anxiety, mood, and substance use disorders: Results from the WHO World Mental Health (WMH) surveys.' *Psychological Medicine 48,* 9, 1560–1571.

Gilbert, P. (2009) *The Compassionate Mind: Compassion-Focussed Therapy.* Robinson.

Greenberger, D. and Padesky, C. (2015) *Mind Over Mood: Change How You Feel by Changing the Way You Think.* The Guildford Press.

Halliwell, E. (2010) *Mindfulness... Report 2010.* London: Mental Health Foundation.

Harris, R. (2019) *ACT Made Simple: An Easy-to-Read Primer on Acceptance and Commitment Therapy.* New Harbinger Publications.

Hayes, L. and Carriochi, J. (2015) *The Thriving Adolescent: Using Acceptance and Commitment Therapy and Positive Psychology to Help Teens Manage Emotions, Achieve Goals and Build Connection.* New Harbinger.

Ho, M. Y., Cheung, F. M. and Cheung, S. F. (2010) 'The role of meaning in life and optimism in promoting well-being.' *Personality and Individual Differences 48,* 5, 658–663.

Kessler, R. C., Berglund, P., Demler, O., Jin, R., Merikangas, K. R. and Walters, E. E. (2005) 'Lifetime prevalence and age-of-onset distributions of DSM-IV disorders in the National Comorbidity Survey Replication.' *Archives of General Psychiatry 62,* 6, 593–602.

Mandalia, D., Ford, T., Hill, S., Sadler, K., *et al.* (2018) *Mental Health of Children and Young People in England, 2017: Professional Services, Informal Support, and Education.* Accessed on 5/8/21 at https://digital.nhs.uk/data-and-information/publications/statistical/mental-health-of-children-and-young-people-in-england/2017/2017.

NICE (2014) *Anxiety Disorders.* Quality standard [QS53]. Accessed on 5/8/21 at www.nice.org.uk/guidance/qs53.

NICE (2019) *Depression in Children and Young People: Identification and Management.* NICE guideline [NG134]. Accessed on 5/8/21 at www.nice.org.uk/guidance/ng134.

Oulasvirta, A., Rattenbury, T., Ma, L. and Raita, E. (2012) 'Habits make smartphone use more pervasive.' *Personal and Ubiquitous Computing 16,* 105–114.

Pass, L., Lejuez, C. and Reynolds, S. (2018) 'Brief Behavioural Activation (Brief BA) for adolescent depression: A pilot study.' *Behavioural and Cognitive Psychotherapy 46,* 2, 182–194.

Reynolds, S. and Pass, L. (2020) *Brief Behavioural Activation for Adolescent Depression: A Clinician's Manual and Session-by-Session Guide.* Jessica Kingsley Publishers.
Sadler, K., Vizard, T., Ford, T., Goodman, A., Goodman, R. and McManus, S. (2018) *Mental Health of Children and Young People in England, 2017: Trends and Characteristics.* NHS Digital.

Find Support and Help

Books and further reading

Beaumont, E. and Welford, M. (2020) *The Kindness Workbook: Creative and Compassionate Ways to Boost Your Wellbeing*. Robinson.

Curran, A. (2019) *The Little Book of Big Stuff about the Brain*. Gomer Press.

Plummer, D. (2014) *Helping Adolescents and Adults to Build Self-Esteem*. Jessica Kingsley Publishers.

Reynolds, S. and Parkinson, M. (2015) *Am I Depressed and What Can I Do About It? A CBT Self-Help Guide for Teenagers Experiencing Low Mood and Depression*. Robinson.

Seiler, L. (2020) *Cool Connections CBT Workbook*. Jessica Kingsley Publishers.

Collins-Donnelly, K. (2013) *Starving the Anxiety Gremlin: A Cognitive Behavioural Therapy Workbook on Anxiety Management for Young People*. Jessica Kingsley Publishers.

Wellbeing books on prescription scheme: https://reading-well.org.uk/books/books-on-prescription/young-people-mental-health.

Mental health and wellbeing support websites

Childline: Online and telephone support for anyone under 19 in the UK with any issue they're going through: www.childline.org.

The Mix: Free, confidential helpline service for young people under 25 who need help but don't know where to turn: www.themix.org.uk/mental-health.

Papyrus: Support to prevent suicide in young people or for people worried about a young person under 35: www.papyrus-uk.org.

Young Minds: UK charity providing information and resources for young people, parents and teachers: www.youngminds.org.uk.

Samaritans: The Samaritans provides a free service for under-18s who need to seek help or support in a crisis: www.samaritans.org.

Togetherall: Online mental health and wellbeing service offering self-help programmes and community support: https://togetherall.com/en-gb.

Kooth: Online counselling and emotional wellbeing for young people: www.kooth.com.

Learn about mental health and wellbeing online

The Association for Child and Adolescent Mental Health: Information about all aspects of mental health and wellbeing: www.acamh.org.

Every Mind Matters: Self-care tips for young people: www.nhs.uk/every-mind-matters/mental-wellbeing-tips/youth-mental-health.

Royal College of Psychiatrists: Information for young people, parents and carers about young people's mental health: www.rcpsych.ac.uk/mental-health/parents-and-young-people.

Apps

BlueIce: Free app to help young people manage their emotions and reduce urges to self-harm: www.oxfordhealth.nhs.uk/blueice.

Calm Harm: Free app to reduce self-harm: https://calmharm.co.uk.

distrACT: Information and advice about self-harm and suicidal thoughts: www.expertselfcare.com/health-apps/distract.

In Hand: Free app helping people focus on the here and now and bring back the balance in a moment of stress or low mood: www.inhand.org.uk.

MeeToo: A safe and secure forum for teenagers wanting to discuss any issue affecting their lives: www.meetoo.help.

Healthy habits websites

Healthy eating: www.bda.uk.com/food-health/food-facts/adolescent-food-facts.html and www.nhs.uk/live-well/eat-well/healthy-eating-for-teens.

Physical activity: www.nhs.uk/live-well/exercise/physical-activity-guidelines-children-and-young-people.

Sleep advice: https://sleepcouncil.org.uk/advice-support/sleep-advice/common-sleep-scenarios/sleep-advice-for-teenagers.

Useful video clips

The hand model of the brain, Professor Dan Siegel: www.youtube.com/watch?v=gm9CIJ74Oxw.

Managing Stress, Brainsmart BBC: www.youtube.com/watch?v=hnpQrMqDoqE.

The Hardwiring of the Brain, Professor Andrew Curran: www.youtube.com/watch?v=p6t8GKdBX04.